Women's Artistic Gymnastics
Handbook

by Elizabeth P. Danskin

ISBN 0-88839-045-9

Copyright © 1983 Danskin, Elizabeth P.

These books have been prepared for the Ministry of Education, Province of British Columbia, under the direction of the Secondary Physical Education Curriculum Revision Committee (1980).

    James Appleby John Lowther
    Alex Carre   Mike McKee
    Madeline Gemmill Norman Olenick
    Gerry Gilmore   David Turkington
    George Longstaff

Handbook Consultant: F. Alex Carre, Ph.D.

Canadian Cataloguing in Publication Data

Danskin, Elizabeth P.
  Women's gymnastics and curriculum guide
(Physical education series)

  ISBN 0-88839-045-9
  1. Gymnastics for Women - Study and teaching.
I. Title. II. Series: Physical Education Series
(Hancock House)
GV464.D35 796.4'1'07' C81-091140-X

All rights reserved. No part of this publication may be reproduced, stored in a retrieval system or transmitted in any form or by any means, electronic, mechanical, photocopying, recording or otherwise without the prior written permission of Hancock House Publishers.

Editor Margaret Campbell
Design Lisa Smedman
Cover Photo Peter Burakoff
Typeset by Lisa Smedman, Diane Pearson & Elizabeth Grant *in Megaron type on an AM Varityper Comp/Edit*
Production Elizabeth Grant, Lois Jobb
Printed in Canada

 *Published by*
HANCOCK HOUSE PUBLISHERS LTD.
19313 Zero Avenue, Surrey, B.C. Canada V3S 5J9

Table of Contents

Acknowledgements 8

Chapter One

Format and Purpose of the Handbook
- A. What is Gymnastics? 9
- B. Purpose of the Handbook 9
- C. Handbook Format 9
- D. Objectives of the Program 9
- E. Application to Classroom Instruction 10
- F. Description of the Levels Approach 10
- G. Explanation of Activity Sequence Chart 11
- H. Activity Sequence Chart 11
- I. Relationship of Women's Artistic Gymnastics to Goals and Learning Outcomes 12

Chapter Two

Preparation
- A. Safety and General Spotting Techniques 13
    1. General Safety Guidelines for the Instructor 13
    2. General Safety Guidelines for the Gymnast 13
    3. Spotting 14
- B. Apparatus 15
- C. Warm-Up and Conditioning Programs 16
    1. Warm-Up 17
    2. Conditioning Exercises 17
    3. Mass Tumbling 18
    4. Dance 18
- D. Teaching the Skill 20
    1. Gradual and Sequential Progression 20
    2. Demonstration 20
    3. Repetition 20
    4. Feedback 20
- E. Classroom Organization 20

Chapter Three

Skill Development and Teaching Techniques
- A. Floor Exercise 21
    - General Safety 21
    - Level I Skills 22
    1. Basic Body Positions 22
    2. Forward Roll-Tuck 22
    3. Backward Roll-Tuck 23
    4. Backward Roll-Straddle 24
    5. Headstand 24
    6. Handstand (with spotting) 25

Level II Skills 27
　　　　7. Forward Roll-Straddle 27
　　　　8. Handstand (three seconds) 27
　　　　9. Cartwheel 28
　　　　10. Chasse 29
　　　　11. Waltz Step 29
　　　　12. Arabesque Hop 29
　　　　13. Body Wave 30
　　　　14. Turns on One Foot 30
　　　Level III Skills 30
　　　　15. Headspring on a Rolled Mat 30
　　　　16. Handstand to Forward Roll 31
　　　　17. Backward Roll to Extension (Handstand) 32
　　　　18. Cartwheel Series 32
　　　　19. Round-Off 33
　　　　20. Round-Off Backward Roll to a Knee Scale 34
　　　　21. Split Leap 34
　　　　22. Sissone 35
　　　　23. Tour Jete 35
　　　　24. Routine 35
　　　Level IV Skills 36
　　　　25. Headspring 36
　　　　26. One-Armed Cartwheel 36
　　　　27. Front Walkover 37
　　　　28. Back Walkover 38
　　　　29. Back and Front Walkovers in Series 39
　　　　30. Handspring 40
　　　　31. Handspring Walkout 40
　　　　32. Valdez 41
　　　　33. Back Handspring 42
　　　　34. Round-Off Back Handspring 43
　　　　35. Optional Routine 44
　B. Uneven Parallel Bars 44
　　　General Safety 44
　　　Level I Skills 45
　　　　1. Long Hang 45
　　　　2. Front Support Mount (Low Bar) 46
　　　　3. Rear Dismount 46
　　　　4. Straddle over Low Bar to Stand 47
　　　Level II Skills 48
　　　　5. Pullover Mount to Front Support (Low Bar) 48
　　　　6. Front Support to Stride Support 48
　　　　7. Straddle Underswing Dismount 49
　　　　8. Front Support Swing (Cast) 50
　　　　9. Back Hip Circle 51
　　　Level III Skills 51
　　　　10. Single Knee Drop and Back to Stride Support 51
　　　　11. Stride Circle Forward 52
　　　　12. Stride Circle Re-Grasp (High Bar) 53

13. Pullover to High Bar 54
14. Pike Drop from High Bar to Low Bar 55
15. Double Leg Stem Rise to High Bar 55
16. Cast from High Bar to Feint Wrap on Low Bar 56
17. Thigh Pivot Turn 58
18. Routine 59
Level IV Skills 59
19. Front Hip Circle 59
20. Single Leg Stem Rise 60
21. Cast from High Bar to Wrap Around Low Bar 60
22. Optional Routine 61

C. Balance Beam 62
   General Safety 62
   Level I Skills 62
    1. Forward Walking 62
    2. Backward Walking 63
    3. Front Support Mount to Stand 63
    4. Knee Scale 64
    5. Two-Foot Jumps 64
    6. One-Half Turn on Toes of Two Feet 64
    7. Forward Roll with Spotting 65
    8. Straight Jump Dismount 66
   Level II Skills 67
    9. Chassé 67
   10. Running Forward 67
   11. Straddle Mount 67
   12. Lunge 68
   13. Changement 68
   14. Tuck Jump 68
   15. One-Half Turn on Toes of One Foot 68
   16. Squat Turn 69
   17. Back Shoulder Roll 69
   18. Straddle Jump Dismount 70
   Level III Skills 70
   19. Squat Mount 70
   20. Single Leg Mount to Squat Position 71
   21. Bent Knee Pose 71
   22. Arabesque 72
   23. Sissone 72
   24. Scissors Leap 72
   25. Kick Turn 72
   26. Forward Roll 73
   27. Backward Roll 73
   28. Round-Off Dismount 74
   29. Routine 74
   Level IV Skills 75
   30. Step On End Mount 75
   31. Forward Roll Mount 76
   32. Splits 76

33. Split Leap 76
  34. Full Turn 77
  35. Continuous Forward Roll 77
  36. Cartwheel 77
  37. Front Walkover 78
  38. Back Walkover 79
  39. Optional Routine 79
 D. Vault 80
   General Safety 80
   Teaching Techniques Common to All Vaults 80
   Level I Skills 82
   1. Squat Vault 82
   Level II Skills 83
   2. Straddle Vault 83
   Level III Skills 83
   3. Layout Squat 83
   Level IV Skills 84
   4. Layout Straddle Vault 84
   5. Stoop Vault 84
   6. Handspring 85
 E. Rules and Basic Judging 87
   1. Judges 87
   2. Compulsory and Optional Exercises 87
   3. Rules for Specific Events 87

Chapter Four
Planning the Program
  A. Organizing the Class 89
    1. Use a Consistent Format 89
    2. Use of Stations 89
    3. Co-ed Classes 89
  B. Lesson Plans 89
  Lesson One: Introduction 90
  Lesson Two: Tumbling and Floor Exercise 91
  Lesson Three: Uneven Parallel Bars 91
  Lesson Four: Balance Beam 92
  Lesson Five: Vault 92
  Lesson Six: "Trouble Clinics"—Skill Testing 93
  Lesson Seven: Written Test 94
  Lesson Eight: Additional Skills on Apparatus — Skill Testing ... 94
  Lesson Nine: Dance and Skill Testing 95
  Lesson Ten: Free Time and Skill Testing 95
0027C. Multi-Levelled Classes 96
0027D. Modified Programs 97

Chapter Five
Evaluation
    A. Introduction 98
    B. Individual Evaluation 98
    C. Program Evaluation 100

Appendix I	Reference Material	101
Appendix II	Personal Gymnastics Booklet	102
Appendix III	Sample Warm-Up	112
Appendix IV	Glossary	116

Acknowledgments

To the Ministry of Education, Curriculum Development Branch, Province of British Columbia, for initiating and developing the Secondary Physical Education Curriculum and Resources Guide, of which this handbook is an integral part.

To Linda Johnstone for her help and constant encouragement.

To Gerry Carr for his advice and for sharing the benefit of his experience.

To the many gymnasts I have taught, coached or judged who have been the force behind my search for "the *best* method."

To Natascha Taft and Margaret Loos for the graphics.

To the gymnasts at Lansdowne Junior Secondary School and to Terry Mack for performing the skills illustrated in this handbook.

To Ken Lundeen, Danny Danskin, Terry Costain and Judy Brumwell for assisting with the photography.

Chapter One
Format And Purpose Of The Handbook

A. Introduction: What is Artistic Gymnastics?

The Canadian Gymnastics Federation states that the term "gymnastics" includes five major areas. These are Artistic Gymnastics, Modern Rhythmic Gymnastics, Trampoline, Educational Gymnastics, Recreational Gymnastics.

Artistic Gymnastics refers to Olympic gymnastics and involves four events for women: Floor Exercise, Uneven Parallel Bars, Balance Beam, and Vault. In competition, gymnasts perform optional and compulsory routines in these events.

Modern Rhythmic Gymnastics is a form of gymnastics done by women only. Gymnasts use light hand apparatus such as ribbons, ropes, hoops, clubs, and balls.

Educational Gymnastics can be thought of as "movement education" involving a variety of movements and using a creative or self-directed approach.

Recreational Gymnastics can be a combination of any of the above forms of gymnastics, presented in an atmosphere that enables the individual to become involved in gymnastics in a positive way.

This handbook covers the events and skills of Artistic Gymnastics, within a Recreational Gymnastics atmosphere. The primary emphasis is on a class instructional program. The skills selected for this handbook have been chosen with the interest and ability level of the average secondary school girl in mind. Many of the skills have been modified so that they provide a challenge to participants. In addition, foundational skills that are necessary background to the higher levels of gymnastics are included.

B. Purpose of the Handbook

This handbook is an extension of the Physical Education Curriculum and Resource Guide (1980). The material presented in the handbook is designed to provide the instructor with a comprehensive source of information for the teaching of Women's Artistic Gymnastics.

C. Handbook Format

This handbook describes in detail the skills required for Women's Artistic Gymnastics. These skills are outlined in the activity sequence chart and categorized according to difficulty to further assist the inexperienced instructor in selecting appropriate skills for the various abilities found in the classroom. Each skill is illustrated and described, and teaching techniques and observation points are discussed. Progressions and spotting procedures are also included.

Ten sample lesson plans are presented to assist the instructor with managing large groups. Specific teaching strategies are discussed throughout. Evaluation and testing methods are presented, as well as suggestions for safety and conditioning.

D. Objectives of the Program

A well-conducted gymnastics unit will meet the objectives of any Physical Education program by enhancing the basic components of fitness such as power, strength, flexibility, balance, coordination, and endurance.

In addition, this sport provides certain psychological benefits associated with feelings of satisfaction and accomplishment which result when you are able to perform a skill well, after a degree of perseverance. The very nature of gymnastics provides an opportunity for its participants to demonstrate courage, creativity, discipline, assurance, and enjoyment. Cooperation and teamwork is attainable through spotting practices, peer teaching, and putting equipment up and down.

The objectives of Artistic Gymnastics are presented under the following categories:

1. **Psychomotor Objectives**

    a) Participants should develop a physically fit body.
    b) Participants should develop cardiovascular endurance, muscular strength, flexibility, balance, and coordination.
    c) Participants should develop effective motor skills which emphasize rhythm, timing and a sense of spatial and body awareness.
    d) Participants should develop an ability to perform spotting skills appropriate to individual capabilities.

2. **Cognitive Objectives**

    a) Participants should develop an understanding and appreciation of the value of Artistic Gymnastics.
    b) Participants should develop an understanding of the different forms of gymnastics and their historical development.
    c) Participants should develop an understanding of the importance of the particular safety precautions specific to the sport of gymnastics.

d) Participants should develop an understanding of the proper maintenance and use of gymnastics apparatus and equipment.
e) Participants should develop an understanding of the proper techniques of routine choreography and the basic rules of judging.

3. Affective Objectives

a) Participants should develop a positive attitude to Artistic Gymnastics through enthusiastic involvement.
b) Participants should develop an awareness of their capabilities and limitations through the performing and spotting of gymnastics skills.
c) Participants should develop an awareness of the needs of other people through cooperation, spotting, and sharing of equipment.
d) Participants should develop an appreciation of the rhythm and gracefulness of dance and artistic gymnastics.
e) Participants should develop positive responses to success and failure in performing skills and routines.
f) Participants should develop perseverance, self-discipline, courage, self-expression, and creativity through the building and performing of skills and routines.

E. Application to Classroom Teaching

For many instructors, the management of a large group of students in a gymnastics class is a difficult task. There is no doubt that this sport requires a good deal of organization and control. If the instructor is well prepared and the students are aware of the objectives of the unit, Women's Artistic Gymnastics will be a very rewarding activity for both the students and the instructor.

It is important to keep in mind, however, that the teaching of gymnastics in the school is quite different from recreational or club coaching. This is due, in part, to the following factors:

1. Many students take gymnastics as a required part of the school program whereas club gymnasts take it by choice and are usually gifted in this area.
2. Students participate for a limited period of time whereas club gymnasts train all year round.
3. The average secondary school girl is weaker than the trained club gymnast, especially in the arms, shoulders and abdomen.
4. The average secondary school girl is usually older than the club gymnast and is experiencing maturational changes which often contribute to strength reduction and weight and flexibility modifications.

F. Description of the Levels Approach

In a comprehensive Physical Education curriculum, emphasis should be placed on the provision of a sound process for individual development. One means of accomplishing this is to utilize a sequentially developed program of physical activities that integrates the affective, cognitive, and psychomotor domains. This focus on individual development is called the "levels" approach.

Each level introduces and develops a certain number of fundamental skills. These skills are the "lead-up" skills to the following level. This allows the participants to progress at their own rate in a safe and logical manner.

Women's Artistic Gymnastics uses a four-level system as follows:

LEVEL I — Beginner — Introduction to the basic movement patterns of gymnastics.
LEVEL II — Novice — Continued development of skills sequential to Level I.
LEVEL III — Intermediate — Introduction to routines, continued development of skills, refinement of basic skills.
LEVEL IV — Advanced — Emphasis on routines developed by participants, refinement of skills from lower levels and exposure to more advanced skills.

At each of the four levels, there are certain skills or activities which can be seen as "the basic requirements." It is suggested that participants must master these skills before proceeding to the next level. This is the minimum requirement.

Levels I and II are designed for the average gymnast in the Physical Education class, while Levels III and IV are generally more appropriate for the better performer such as the gymnast who is able to spend additional time working on gymnastics through outside clubs or extra-curricular activities.

The Canadian Gymnastics Federation's Development Program has also established a levels approach to teaching gymnastic skills. Book I *Participation* contains three levels, Red, White and Blue. Instructors wishing direction in choosing skills prior to Level I of this handbook should refer to C.G.F.'s Book I. Book II, *Men's Achievement*, and Book III, *Women's Achievement*, contain four additional levels, Merit, Bronze, Silver and Gold. Instructors requiring additional skills after Level IV of this handbook should refer to C.G.F.'s Silver and Gold Levels. Levels I - IV of this handbook are closely related to C.G.F. White, Blue, Merit and Bronze levels.

G. Explanation of the Activity Sequence Chart

The activity sequence chart outlines a progressive pattern of skills for the four events of Women's Artistic Gymnastics. The chart serves as a guide in planning sessions and indicates the level at which each skill might be introduced.

H. Activity Sequence Chart

A. Floor Exercises

Skills	I	II	III	IV
1. Basic Body Positions	•			
2. Forward Roll — Tuck	•			
3. Backward Roll — Tuck	•			
4. Backward Roll — Straddle	•			
5. Headstand	•			
6. Handstand (with spotting)	•			
7. Forward Roll — Straddle		•		
8. Handstand (3 seconds)		•		
9. Cartwheel		•		
10. Chassé		•		
11. Waltz Step		•		
12. Arabesque Hop		•		
13. Body Wave		•		
14. Turns on One Foot		•		
15. Headspring on a Rolled Mat			•	
16. Handstand to Forward Roll			•	
17. Backward Roll to Extension (Handstand)			•	
18. Cartwheel Series			•	
19. Round-off			•	
20. Round-off Backward Roll to a Knee Scale			•	
21. Split Leap			•	
22. Sissone			•	
23. Tour Jêté			•	
24. Routine			•	
25. Headspring				•
26. One-armed Cartwheel				•
27. Front Walkover				•
28. Back Walkover				•
29. Back and Front Walkovers in Series				•
30. Handspring				•
31. Handspring Walkout				•
32. Valdez				•
33. Back Handspring				•
34. Round-off Back Handspring				•
35. Optional Routine				•

B. Uneven Parallel Bars

Skills	I	II	III	IV
1. Long Hang	•			
2. Front Support Mount (low bar)	•			
3. Rear Dismount	•			
4. Straddle Over Low Bar to Stand	•			
5. Pullover Mount to Front Support (low bar)		•		
6. Front Support Swing to Stride Support		•		
7. Straddle Underswing Dismount		•		
8. Front Support Swing (Cast)		•		
9. Back Hip Circle		•		
10. Single Knee Drop and Back to Stride Support			•	
11. Stride Circle Forward			•	
12. Stride Circle Re-grasp (High Bar)			•	
13. Pullover to High Bar			•	
14. Pike Drop From High Bar to Low Bar			•	
15. Double Leg Stem Rise to High Bar			•	
16. Cast From High Bar to Feint Wrap on Low Bar			•	
17. Thigh Pivot Turn			•	
18. Routine			•	
19. Front Hip Circle				•
20. Single Leg Stem Rise				•
21. Cast From High Bar to Wrap Around Low Bar				•
22. Optional Routine				•

SKILLS	LEVELS			
	I	II	III	IV
C. Balance Beam				
1. Forward Walking	●			
2. Backward Walking	●			
3. Front Support Mount to Stand	●			
4. Knee Scale	●			
5. Two-foot Jumps	●			
6. One-Half Turn on Toes of Two Feet	●			
7. Forward Roll With Spotting	●			
8. Straight Jump Dismount	●			
9. Chassé		●		
10. Running Forward		●		
11. Straddle Mount		●		
12. Lunge		●		
13. Changement		●		
14. Tuck Jump		●		
15. One-half Turn on Toes of One Foot		●		
16. Squat Turn		●		
17. Back Shoulder Roll		●		
18. Straddle Jump Dismount		●		
19. Squat Mount			●	
20. Single Leg Mount to Squat Position			●	
21. Bent Knee Pose			●	
22. Arabesque			●	
23. Sissone			●	
24. Scissors Leap			●	
25. Kick Turn			●	
26. Forward Roll			●	
27. Backward Roll			●	
28. Round-off Dismount			●	
29. Routine			●	
30. Step On End Mount				●
31. Forward Roll Mount				●
32. Splits				●
33. Split Leap				●
34. Full Turn				●
35. Continuous Forward Roll				●
36. Cartwheel				●
37. Front Walkover				●
38. Back Walkover				●
39. Optional Routine				●
D. Vault				
1. Squat Vault	●			
2. Straddle Vault		●		
3. Layout Squat			●	
4. Layout Straddle Vault				●
5. Stoop Vault				●
6. Handspring				●

I. Relationship of Women's Artistic Gymnastics to Goals and Learning Outcomes

A series of Goals and Learning Outcomes for physical education were developed for the Secondary Physical Education Curriculum and Resource Guide (1980). The relationship of Women's Artistic Gymnastics to the four major goals of this Curriculum Guide is indicated below.

1. Participants should demonstrate increased physical fitness in terms of power, strength, flexibility, coordination, and endurance.
2. Participants should demonstrate a development of efficient and effective motor skills.
3. Participants should demonstrate a greater understanding of the sport of Artistic Gymnastics as an expressive art form.
4. Participants should demonstrate improvement in such qualities as courage, creativity, discipline, and initiative. They should demonstrate an ability to work cooperatively with others, and display a positive and enthusiastic attitude toward Artistic Gymnastics.

Chapter Two
Preparation

A. Safety and General Spotting Techniques

Safety and liability is a topic that has serious implications for the gymnastics instructor. The use of unyielding apparatus and the many body positions involved in gymnastics increase the element of risk. However, the instructor can control the risk inherent in gymnastics by emphasizing appropriate safety techniques.

An instructor must "act as a reasonably prudent person would act." This means:
1. The gymnastics activity must be suitable for the age and condition of the student.
2. The student must be progressively trained.
3. The equipment must be safe, suitably arranged, and appropriate to the skill level of the student.
4. The activity must be properly supervised.

In addition, it is the responsibility of the instructor to educate gymnasts as to what their responsibilities are. They should know the proper use and care of equipment; the correct spotting techniques; and the responsibilities that go with spotting. Each gymnast should be aware of her physical limitations and work within them. She should understand the importance of progressing from the basics and working up to the more advanced skills. General safety rules should be discussed and the students made aware that they have a responsibility for their own safety as well.

1. General Safety Guidelines For the Instructor

a) *The instructor should be the first one in the gymnasium and the last one to leave when gymnastics equipment is set up.*

Students should be instructed that no one goes on the apparatus until the instructor is in the gymnasium. The instructor must position herself so she can see the activity of the entire class. She should make a point of circulating around the gymnasium to all events or stations.

b) *All teaching must be progressive.*

Instructors should be aware of the stages and lead-ups to a particular skill. This allows the instructor and the gymnast to see the particular limitations of the gymnast and proceed in a safe manner. The levels system used in this handbook is one form of progression. Where applicable, teaching progressions for the skills are discussed in Chapter Three.

c) *Work within your own physical limitations, knowledge, and training.*

Do not let yourself be talked into teaching or spotting skills with which you are not comfortable. It is far better to offer a good basic course than to allow the students to move ahead on their own to the advanced skills without adequate instruction.

Stop when you are fatigued and don't be talked into spotting "just one more." If the gymnast must constantly rely on spotting, she is obviously not ready and should go back to the preceding progression.

d) *Stress safety throughout your unit.*

On the first day, when the unit is being introduced, discuss the safety rules that you expect your gymnasts to follow. A copy of these rules should be made available to each student. When the equipment is being introduced for the first time, have the students sit down and take notes while the skills are demonstrated and introduced. The specific safety practices, progressions, and spotting should be discussed.

e) *Be sure the equipment is maintained and used in a safe manner.*

When Artistic Gymnastics apparatus is used, there should always be mats covering the supports, and the floor under and around the apparatus. Mats should not overlap and should be positioned so they do not slip. Be sure adjustable apparatus is secure before the class begins. Defective apparatus must not be used. Areas for mounting and dismounting from the apparatus must be provided and kept clear. An overcrowded, disorganized gymnasium is a hazard.

2. General Safety Guidelines For the Gymnast

a) Do not wear jewelery to class.
b) Tie long hair back and keep loose hair from falling in your face.
c) Be sure you are warmed up before proceeding to the apparatus. Only you know if you are adequately warmed up and ready to attempt more difficult skills.
d) Be sure adjustable apparatus is secure and set at a height and distance you are used to.
e) Check that there are adequate mats surrounding the apparatus and that they are not overlapping.

f) Avoid loose or tight clothing that restricts movement. A leotard is ideal. Slippery footwear must be avoided.
g) Do not work out when you are ill or fatigued.
h) Be sure your spotter is competent and aware of which skill you are performing.
i) Master the basics before proceeding to the more advanced skills.
j) Avoid "horseplay."
k) Observe all safety rules.
l) Don't work out in an unsupervised gymnasium.

3. Spotting

Spotting is a skill in itself. It can be done with just a hand contact or may involve actually lifting the gymnast through the entire movement. Spotting can be done with mechanical devices such as the spotting belt, or it can be just readiness to assist if necessary.

In a class of thirty gymnasts it is impossible for the instructor to attempt to do all the spotting. In addition, the students are missing out on a very valuable and rewarding aspect of gymnastics if they are not taught spotting techniques. Spotting must be taught progressively just as the skills are taught progressively. However, students should be used as spotters only in circumstances where they have the strength and ability to support the weight of fellow students.

Spotters should know the *techniques* of the skill before they attempt to spot it. Both the gymnast and the spotter should know how the spotting is to be done. Spotters should be made aware that they have a responsibility for the safety of their gymnast. Students very often take this responsibility very lightly and need to be reminded that the gymnast is depending on them for her safety.

Common Spotting Errors

a) Too much expected of the spotter.

It is important to match size in selecting partners for spotting. Spotters should not attempt to spot gymnasts who are much larger than they are.

It is very strenuous lifting an unskilled gymnast through a skill. The gymnast should not expect the spotter to do the skill for her. She must have completed all the progressions prior to doing a particular skill.

Most importantly, a spotter must have knowledge of the *techniques* to performing a skill before she can spot it. It is not always necessary that she be able to perform it but she must be familiar with how it is done.

b) Lack of communication between the gymnast and the spotter.

The gymnast must discuss what she is about to perform and how she expects to be spotted. It is unreasonable for the gymnast to assume that the spotter knows how much or how little assistance she requires.

There must also be communication between the spotters if there is more than one. They must know exactly what each is doing and not assume anything.

c) Spotter positions herself too far from the gymnast to be effective.

Beginning spotters tend to feel safest when they are not too close to the gymnast.

Spotters must commit themselves to the responsibility of spotting and position themselves in the most effective manner. A straight arm extended in an effort to spot a back handspring is of little use. A flexed arm close to the gymnast, so the shoulder is involved, is much more effective.

The top of a Swedish box is a very useful apparatus for spotting skills where the gymnast is some distance above the spotters. Standing on the box allows for better contact and leverage.

d) Lower back spotting.

It is a natural reaction to reach for the back in spotting many of the flexibility skills. However, lifting the body weight at the lower back can place considerable stress on the spine. It is far safer to place the hand on the upper back or the hips.

It is important to remember that a woman's center of gravity is lower than a man's and in most instances most of the weight is in the hips. As long as the hips are guided properly, the gymnast will be controlled and in most cases will remain on the apparatus.

e) Overspotting.

With proper communication this should not occur. The spotter must also assess the weight of the gymnast so she does not accidentally "throw" her through the skill.

As the gymnast becomes more competent, the spotter must gradually reduce the amount of assistance so the gymnast will learn to perform the skill on her own. If the spotter overspots, the gymnast never really "feels" the skill and tends to become dependent on the spotter. It is important to have the gymnast performing on her own so you are able to move away and view the entire skill from a distance. Technique corrections are difficult to see while spotting in close.

f) Lack of confidence between gymnast and spotter.

Never do anything less than you say you will. It is important for the gymnast to be able to rely totally on the spotter.

If the instructor is having difficulty getting a gymnast to try a particular skill on her own, go back to each one of the progressions in turn and work up to doing the skill "solo." Usually the confidence she gets doing the simpler progressions will carry her over to the final performance on her own.

g) Letting go of the gymnast before she is under control.

This error occurs mostly in the early stages of spotting a skill, when the gymnast is not familiar with the movement pattern. This is particularly prevalent in skills involving an inverted body position. Her momentum continues after the spotters have let go. Spotters should follow through until the gymnast is under control.

h) Not moving through the skill with the gymnast.

In those skills that require movement over a distance the spotter must be prepared to move with the gymnast. In the upright position a shuffle or sliding step rather than a cross step is the safest manner of moving with the gymnast.

B. Apparatus

The Federation of International Gymnastics (FIG) has set specific dimensions for standard apparatus, and their suggested dimensions are indicated below:

Apparatus Dimension	Standard	For Classroom Use
Floor Exercise Area	12 m x 12 m (39' x 39')	12 m x 12 m (39' x 39')
Uneven Parallel Bars		
Height of Upper Bar	230 cm (7' 6-1/2")	230 cm (7' 6-1/2")
Height of Lower Bar	150 cm (4' 11")	150 cm (4' 11")
Balance Beam		
Height	120 cm (3' 11-1/4")	100 cm (3' 3")
Length	5 m (16' 4-7/8")	5 m (16' 4-7/8")
Width	10 cm (3-7/8" — usually considered 4")	10 cm (3-7/8" — usually considered 4")
Vaulting Horse		
Height	120 cm (3' 11-1/4')	110 cm (3' 7-1/4") (for horizontal and above) 90 cm (2' 11") (below horizontal)

An example of dimensions which might require modification for classroom use are those for the balance beam and the vaulting horse. A height of 100 cm (3' 3") for the balance beam is more suitable for the non-competitive gymnast. A height of 90 cm (2' 11") for the vaulting horse would be more appropriate for vaults that are performed below the horizontal.

Instructors must be prepared to make such apparatus adjustments according to the ability level and physical size of the participants.

1. Floor Exercise

The official floor exercise area is 12 meters by 12 meters (39' by 39'). However, an adequate covering for this event is a three-piece wrestling mat. This covers a 9 meter by 9 meter (30' by 30') area and can easily accommodate a class of thirty-five students.

When this is not available, one small mat for every three participants will be adequate. In this instance, the participants are not able to do as many repetitions as a long length of mats would allow, but everyone will get sufficient activity.

2. Uneven Parallel Bars

Although there are many ways in which various pieces of apparatus can be modified for this event, a good set of uneven bars that can be *secured to the floor* should be purchased as soon as funds become available. Height and width adjustments can easily be made on proper uneven bars and they are much more stable. The need for safety on uneven parallel bars cannot be over emphasized.

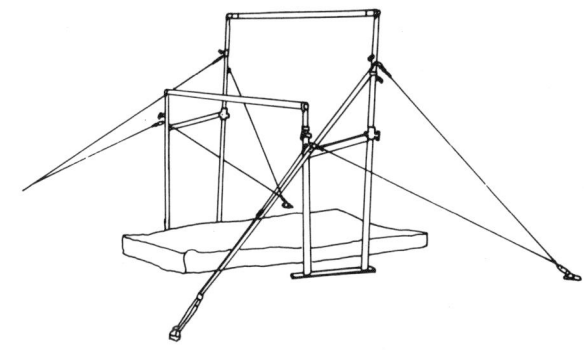

Sufficient mats must be available to cover all supports and to provide a safe landing. Again, a landing pad is ideal.

For those more difficult skills, a towel wrapped around the low bar and secured with tape can provide extra padding to help eliminate bruised hips.

Participants should be encouraged to rub magnesium chalk on their hands to absorb perspiration and reduce the possibilities of slipping.

The beat board is used for many mounts.

3. Balance Beam

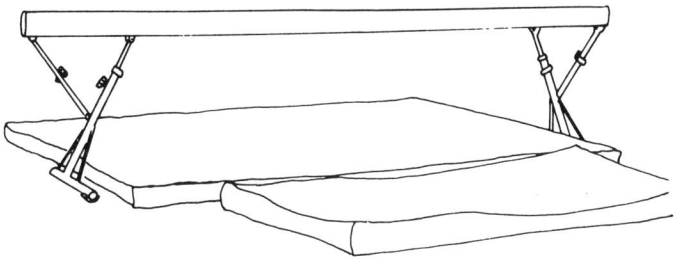

In addition to the standard balance beam, a low practice beam allows participants an opportunity to work on the more difficult skills at a low level.

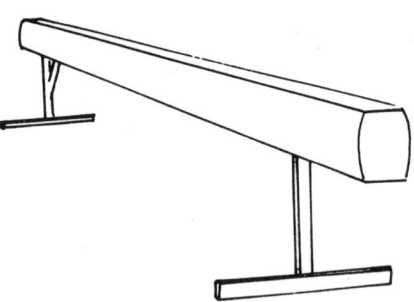

The benches found in most schools can also serve as modified balance beams. Tape can be used to show the proper width of a regulation beam.

The beat board is used for many mounts. Again, as for the other apparatus, there must be sufficient mats to cover the floor and the supports safely. A landing pad is useful for dismounts.

A towel secured by masking tape will also provide extra padding for skills such as the forward roll.

4. Vault

The equipment generally required for this event is a Swedish box, a beat board, and sufficient mats for a safe landing, preferably a landing pad. The Swedish box is particularly useful because of the various levels to which it can be adjusted. It is made up of four sections held in place by wooden pegs. At full height, however, the sloping sides of the Swedish box may create some problems for spotters. The slope tends to keep the spotter away from the gymnast, and difficulties may arise in providing the gymnast with adequate support.

Wear and tear on the wooden pegs may cause the Swedish box to become loose. Ensure that the sections are secure and fit tightly together.

The top section can be very useful for spotting skills on the balance beam and uneven bars. By standing on the top section, the spotter can get the height necessary to give the gymnast proper support.

By using the various levels of the Swedish box, students can begin at a reasonable height and gradually increase the height as they become more confident.

The pommel horse is also used for vaulting. The wooden pommel handles are removed and holes plugged or taped over. There are, however, some restrictions to varying the height. Even at its lowest height, many students find it ominous.

The take-off apparatus, the beat board, is available with or without a covering. The covered beat board is best if it is affordable. It is usually covered with an indoor/outdoor type of carpeting. The carpet provides the gymnast with some cushioning as she hits the board.

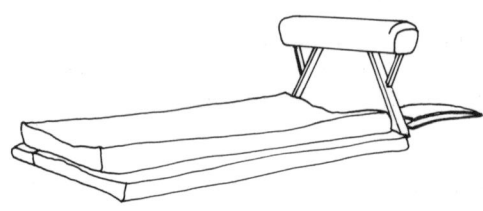

The springboard and trampette are two other forms of take-off apparatus. It is recommended that these two apparatus be used only by very experienced gymnasts because both tend to throw the gymnast.

C. Warm-Up and Conditioning Programs

Such programs are important for the following reasons:
  a) It is during this time that many of the fitness-related goals of the overall Physical Education program can be realized.
  b) They provide mental and physical preparation for more strenuous activity.
  c) They provide an opportunity for flexibility exercises to be stressed. This aspect of general fitness is often neglected in the other activities of the total Physical Education program.
  d) They provide an opportunity for the class to work together as a group before each participant works on individual programs.

A suggested format to include all aspects of warm-up and conditioning might be as follows:
1. Warm-up
2. Conditioning Exercises
3. Mass Tumbling

1. Warm-Up

The value of a warm-up before an athletic event is widely accepted, and all gymnasts should begin workouts with an extensive warm-up.

The warm-up should occupy the first five to ten minutes of a gymnastics class, and include dance and locomotor movements to improve grace and posture.

There is probably no "best" program of specific movements for the gymnastics warm-up, but there are some general principles and suggestions to keep in mind to help make the warm-up an enjoyable and beneficial aspect of the class.

Although the warm-up will vary from day to day, the following approach is recommended:

a) Cardiovascular activities — basic locomotor activities
   Arrange students in a circle.
   A "follow-the-leader" approach works very well.
b) Dance related activities — free swinging, rhythmical exercises, turns, leaps, polka.
c) Individual static stretching — flexibility exercises
   Static stretching should be used at all times. The chance of a pulled muscle is greater with ballistic or "bobbing type" exercises. Encourage the participants to stretch to their maximum *slowly* and *progressively*.
   A scatter formation on the mats or floor can be used for the stretching and conditioning.
d) Conditioning exercises — strength, sit-ups, push-ups

During the first week of the unit, the instructor should lead and explain the specific effect on the body of each exercise. In succeeding weeks, select a different student each day to lead the next day's warm-up. This not only provides participants with an opportunity to demonstrate leadership, but also encourages them to attend to the exercises in case they are called upon to lead the warm-up.

Where feasible, introduce exercises which are different from those used in other Physical Education activities so that the gymnastics warm-up seems special. A wide variety of exercises adds to the appeal of the program. However, the following exercises should form the core of each warm-up:

Running	Backbend or Bridge
Splits	Sit-ups
Push-ups	Jacks or V-sits

All exercises should be performed with the utmost care and attention to correct posture, and "form" or execution. This will have a carry-over effect on other gymnastic skills.

The use of music enhances the warm-up. The music need not be designed to accompany each exercise, but may merely provide background.

Try to have exercises arranged so you proceed easily from one to the other. For instance, do all standing exercises first, all straddle ones together, and so on. The exercises in the sample warm-up (see Appendix III) are ordered with this in mind.

2. Conditioning Exercises

In addition to the warm-up, gymnasts should be involved in a conditioning program. The Canadian Gymnastics Federation states that "conditioning is vital for:
1. reduced incidence of injuries
2. faster and more correct skill acquisition
3. reduced incidence of muscle soreness
4. prolonged period of participation
5. more sustained and intense participation"

The serious gymnast should be involved in a conditioning program emphasizing the following aspects of fitness: endurance (muscular and cardiovascular), strength, power, and flexibility. Programs should be designed with a view to correcting the particular weakness of the individual—for instance, increasing upper body strength.

Conditioning exercises usually follow the gymnastics workout, but in a Physical Education class, conditioning exercises are generally better performed at the end of the warm-up.

a) Sit-ups — Begin with 15, increase to 25 over entire unit.

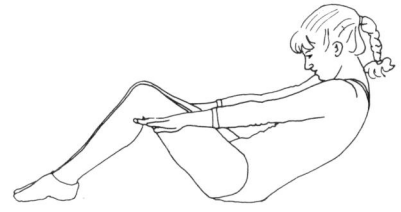

b) Push-ups — Work up to 10.

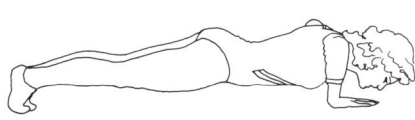

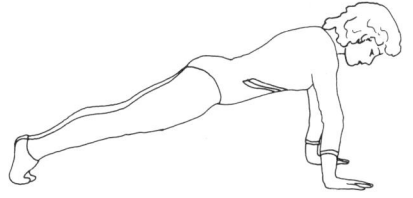

Use full, straight body push-ups. The correct technique should be explained. Girls should be encouraged to work on one or two correct push-ups rather than ten incorrect.

　　c) Jacks or V-Sits — Begin with 5, increase to 15 over entire unit.

　　　Lie on the floor, face up, arms above head, legs together. This is the layout position.

From a layout position, raise arms and legs off the floor to form a pike position or V-sit. Then lower to layout. Legs must be straight throughout.

3. Mass Tumbling

Tumbling is the preliminary conditioner for preparing the gymnast for the other events. A tumbling warm-up done by the entire class after conditioning exercises is referred to as "mass tumbling." It provides an opportunity for an extended warm-up period, a chance to review tumbling skills, a chance to observe how individuals are progressing, and an opportunity for the participants to enjoy a variety of new, different tumbling activities. The skills should be basic, should include an element of review, should be progressive in difficulty, and should require little or no spotting.

Mass tumbling can accommodate all four "levels" at once because the skills are progressive and as the skills become more difficult, participants can drop out and move on to their individual programs. This is also an ideal time to begin introducing simple combinations of tumbling skills: forward roll → ½ turn → backward → straddle roll. Examples of exercises to be used can be found throughout the lesson plans.

4. Dance

A good background in ballet gives a gymnast an excellent start in gymnastics. Gymnastics incorporates many forms of dance, most of which borrow positions and movements from ballet. A gymnast who has some training in dance knows that turning the legs out gives a more pleasing and elegant line when the legs are extended; the use of the arms draws the eye upward to the upper body and head; and that every movement should stress posture and correct body alignment. A knowledge of dance also makes the gymnast familiar with choreography, and teaches her techniques for developing more aesthetically appealing movement patterns.

Dance movements and dance techniques should be included in the warm-up and conditioning programs.

　　a) Basic Ballet Positions

First Position

Feet: Place the heels together, toes pointing away from each other.

Arms: Arms rounded, in front of the body just below the waist. Palms inward.

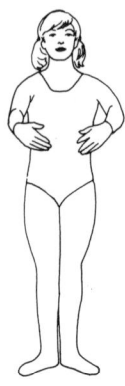

Second Position

Feet: As in first position, heels about one step apart.

Arms: Arms are held to the side, just below shoulder level, and slightly flexed at the elbow. Palms in optional position.

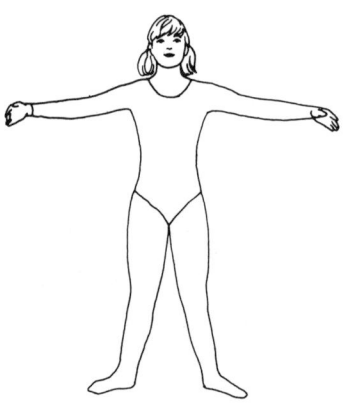

Third Position

Feet: Feet are pressed together so the heel of one foot is at the instep of the other foot. Toes are turned out.

Arms: One arm is raised in a curve over the head, forward of the body. The other arm remains in second position.

Fourth Position

Feet: One foot is in front of the other foot, approximately the distance of one foot. The heel of the forward foot is lined up with the toes of the rear foot.

Arms: One arm is raised above the head as in third position. The other arm is held low in front as in first position.

Fifth Position

Feet: As in fourth position, only feet are pressed together.

Arms: Both arms are raised above the head as in third position. Palms facing downward.

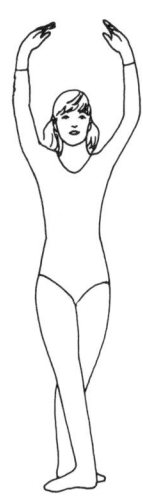

b) Leaps, Jumps and Hops

These basic locomotor skills always begin with a demi-plié, a slight knee bend with the heel off the floor, and end in a demi-plié to absorb shock and allow for a smooth, controlled landing. The take off involves extending the knee, ankle and finally giving a strong push with the toes. The landing is done with the toes first, then the heel. Leaps, hops and jumps must be explosive and show height, yet demonstrate control. The upper body should be erect and full body extension should be evident. The arms should add to the appeal of the movement, appearing relaxed and controlled. Ankles and toes are extended while the body is in the air.

Leap — Take off on one foot, land on the other.
Jump — Two-foot take off.
Hop — Take off and land on the same foot.

c) Turns

Turns are used to change direction and add variety and rhythm changes. Most turns are done on the balls of the feet and the center of gravity must always be over the base of support. Turns should be smooth and continuous. Arms should hold a definite position. Eye spotting will help to keep balanced and prevent dizziness.

D. Teaching the Skill

Skill acquisition in gymnastics is enhanced by giving careful attention to the following instructional considerations:

1. Gradual and Sequential Progression

All skills must be built up from the basic movement patterns to the complex, technically correct performance of the complete skill. This is accomplished through the use of lead-ups or "progressions."

Progressions may involve various aspects of gymnastics besides actual skill modifications. For instance, the change from two spotters to one spotter marks one stage in a gradual progression, as does the change from a "heavy" spot to a "light" spot.

Progressions may also involve modifications of apparatus. For example, a walkover on the balance beam may progress from a walkover on the mats to a line on the floor, to a bench, to a line on a bench, to a low regulation beam with three spotters, to two spotters, to a beam gradually raised to regulation height, and so on.

2. Demonstration

Clear and concise demonstration of what the gymnast is expected to do is essential. There are many methods of demonstrating a skill. The skill can be presented verbally, pictorially, actually, or a combination of all these. A suggested method of demonstrating a skill on the uneven bars to a Level I group might be as follows:

i) Have a student demonstrate the skill.
ii) Discuss the two or three most important aspects.
iii) Demonstrate the skill again showing the correct spotting technique.
iv) Discuss the spotting technique.
v) Demonstrate the skill again.

Resource books can be very helpful for reinforcing the demonstration and assisting those who require additional information.

3. Repetition

Instructors must provide for sufficient repetition, to reinforce skill learning. Only by repetition will the movement pattern be learned. This is especially true of the more complex skills.

4. Feedback

Accurate feedback must be provided. For learning to take place, the gymnast must have feedback, whether it is constructive criticism, positive reinforcement, or any other method of communicating information about a particular performance. When correcting skills, first point out the major errors and then, as the skill becomes more refined, indicate the smaller corrections.

Feedback need not come only from the instructor. Participants should learn to correct and encourage each other.

Video equipment is an invaluable means of providing feedback. Many schools now have video equipment available and it is ideal for use in gymnastics classes. While it may seem time consuming to set up this equipment, the benefits are immeasurable.

E. Classroom Organization

Few activities require more organization than a gymnastics unit. The following list will assist the instructor with the planning:

a) Check the facility in which you will be working. How much space will be available? Determine the boundaries.
b) Check to see what equipment is available.
c) Check that the equipment is in good condition. Put chalk in a container ready for classroom use.
c) Most of the equipment will have to be locked away for safety reasons, but ideally you should arrange for it to be kept close to the teaching area so that the setting up and putting away of the equipment is not too time consuming.
e) Run off handouts for *all* gymnastics classes. You should have a list of safety rules, a set of personal gymnastics booklets (see Appendix II), and copies of the written tests ready before you begin teaching.
f) Read over the lesson plans in Chapter Four and modify according to the number of lessons allotted and your particular experience.
g) Begin familiarizing yourself with the skills, and with the teaching and spotting techniques described in Chapter Three.
h) Gather resource materials for use during class time. Many films and other audio-visual materials must be booked months in advance.
i) Set up the unit so that each class uses the same basic format. In this way students become familiar with the procedure and time used for instruction is minimized. The following format is suggested:
   Equipment set up
   Attendance
   Warm-up, conditioning
   Mass tumbling — review
   New material—demonstrations, note taking
   Culminating activities—students working on individual programs

Chapter Three
Skill Development and Teaching Techniques

The events for Women's Artistic Gymnastics are designed to take into account the lower center of gravity and relatively weak upper body of the female gymnast compared to that of the male. Each event has a special beneficial influence on the complete development of the body. The student who works on all four events is gaining maximum benefit. For this reason it is suggested that the student be exposed to all four events and not be limited to only one or two.

A. Floor Exercise

Regardless of what age group you are working with, every gymnastics unit should begin with the "basics." Depending on the level taught, and the background of your participants, this may be a review, a new learning experience, or a combination of both. After the basics, the students can then progress according to their own abilities. Gymnastics skills must be taught through the proper progressions if learning is to take place in the most effective manner.

The floor exercise event combines tumbling elements with dance movements and provides the basic movement patterns for the other three events. Every gymnastics unit should therefore begin with this event. From the instructor's point of view, there are two other advantages to introducing this event first. It can accommodate the greatest number of students and, because it does not involve apparatus, it does not arouse the fears many girls have about gymnastics, particularly the fear of height.

General Safety

1. It is important to check all mats to see that they do not overlap or slip apart. Where necessary, mats should be taped together to keep from separating. Mats should be clean and free from dust. Firm matting should be used for the floor exercise area with soft absorbent mats or crash pads for landings. Netting with rubber chip filling or other mats where the stuffing moves should not be used.
2. When moving mats, lift them, do not drag them. This increases their life expectancy.
3. Be sure that all participants have sufficient space to perform the tumbling skills. The tumbling area should be free from cables and apparatus.
4. Make tumblers aware that collisions will occur unless the following precautions are taken:

    i) Always work in the same direction if possible.
    ii) Do not follow too closely. A good rule is to begin when the person in front of you has finished their second repetition.
    iii) Watch to see that the person in front of you has not stopped for some reason.
    iv) Skills that require a long running approach should always be performed in the same area.
5. The instructor must choose a position which allows a clear view of the tumbling area.

SKILL	DESCRIPTION	TEACHING TECHNIQUES AND OBSERVATION POINTS

Level I Skills

1. Basic Body Positions

a) Tuck — Sitting on the floor pull knees up to chest and "make yourself as small as possible" by rounding the back. *Clasp knees with arms.*

b) Straddle — From a sitting position on the floor, spread legs as far apart as possible—"make yourself as wide as possible"—arms optional.

c) Pike — From a sitting position on the floor, legs straight and together, bend from the waist "making the body as flat as possible."

d) Layout — From a sitting position, lower the back to the floor and assume a supine position. Legs straight and together.

1. It will assist the learning of these positions if the class assumes each position as the instructor names it during the warm-up.

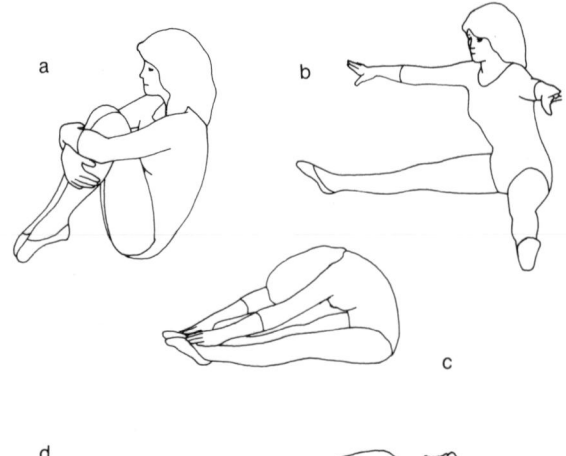

2. Forward Roll — Tuck

1. From a squatting position, reach forward and place hands shoulder width apart on the mat.
2. Follow through with the roll by extending the legs and pushing with the feet, tucking the legs as the hips hit the mat, and coming to a squat position again.

1. Practice tucking the head and extending the legs.
2. Practice gently rocking in a tucked position.
3. Practice the roll from a stand position to a stand.

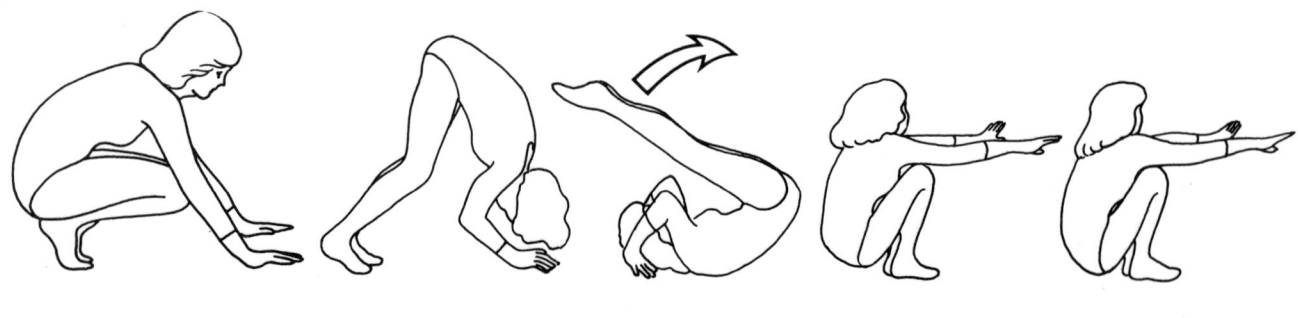

SKILL	DESCRIPTION	TEACHING TECHNIQUES AND OBSERVATION POINTS

Spotting
Initiate the roll by tucking the head under and assist the gymnast to a squat or stand.

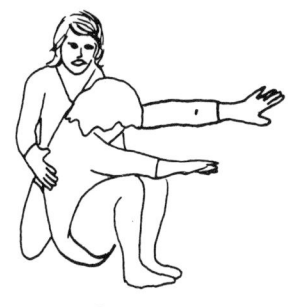

3. Backward Roll — Tuck

1. Assume a deep squat position, knees together, hands partially supporting weight on mat in front of body.
2. Push backwards and immediately place hands on shoulders, palms up.
3. Extend legs until hands touch mat, then tuck legs as toes touch mat above head.
4. Extend arms and come to a squat.

1. Practice gently rocking as in a forward roll.
2. Arms must be used to take weight off neck.
3. Initially a roll to the knees can be executed.
4. Be sure to round back.
5. Push evenly with both hands or roll will be crooked.

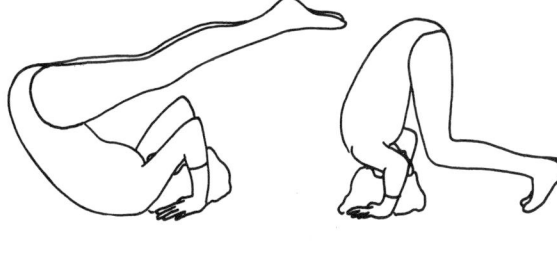

Spotting
Kneel to one side of gymnast; as the hips are brought to overhead position, grasp waist and assist in lifting hips overhead to squat position.

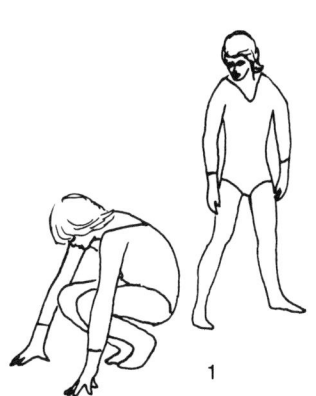

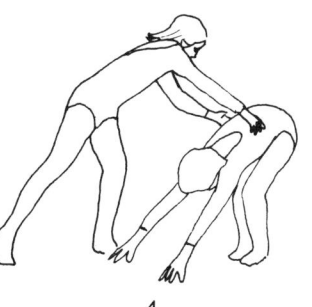

SKILL	DESCRIPTION	TEACHING TECHNIQUES AND OBSERVATION POINTS
4. Backward Roll — Straddle	1. From a straddle stand position, shift hips backward, allowing shoulders to come forward. 2. Hands are placed on floor between legs reaching as far back as possible. The weight is taken on the hands and the hips lowered to the mat. 3. The legs remain wide apart and are brought over the head. Feet are placed on the mat above the head. 4. The hand placement is the same as in the backward roll-tuck, and the arms are extended to place the body back in a straddle stand position.	1. Initially, this roll should be done by performing a backward roll (feet together) and then straddling the legs to a straddle stand. 2. Care must be taken that participants do not land heavily on their tailbones. *Spotting* 1. Assist gymnast with gently lowering to the mat by supporting the hips from the waist. 2. Continue to assist gymnast by spotting as for the backward roll.

 1 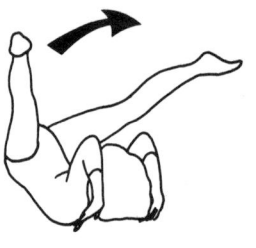 2 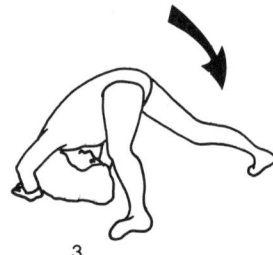 3

5. Headstand	1. Initially the headstand should be done from the tripod or "teddy bear" stand. From the kneeling position, place hands on the mat, shoulder width apart, fingers spread. Place the hairline area of the head on the mat to form an equilateral triangle with the hands. As the hips are raised, the head rolls so that the weight is on the top of the head. Raise the hips by extending the legs and placing one knee at a time on the elbows.	1. Elbows should be steady and not allowed to wiggle. 2. Do not jump into position. 3. Do not allow head to roll. *Spotting* 1. The spotter should stand facing the gymnast's back and place her hands on the gymnast's hips to keep her from overbalancing.

SKILL	DESCRIPTION	TEACHING TECHNIQUES AND OBSERVATION POINTS
	2. From the tripod position, arch back slightly and bring knees together. Extend legs upward to the headstand position. Hold for three seconds and return to tripod.	1. Be sure to keep hips from going past the perpendicular. 2. Keep legs together. 3. Move into and out of the position in a controlled manner. 4. More advanced gymnasts may attempt the headstand from a prone position. *Spotting* 1. The spotter should stand in the same position as for the tripod. 2. Assume a steady stance so as to control the gymnast should she overbalance. 3. Keep head to one side to avoid gymnast's feet.

1

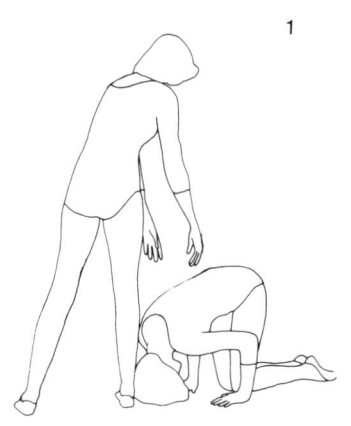  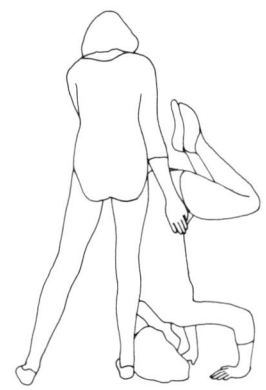 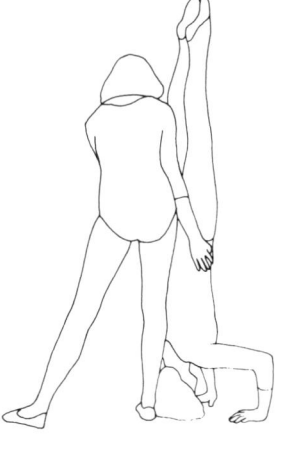

2　　　　　　　　　3　　　　　　　　　4　　　　　　　　　5

6. Handstand (with spotting)	1. Raise the hands over the head, at the same time, raise the right leg. Step forward on the right foot, bending the right knee. 2. Place the hands, fingers spread, shoulder width apart on the mat. (The fingers are used to keep from overbalancing, the same way the toes are.) 3. Swing the left leg backwards and up with the right leg from the floor. 4. Bring legs together in the inverted position.	1. This is one of the most important skills in gymnastics and time spent in helping your students reach a correct handstand position is never wasted. In many other skills the body will pass through the handstand position. 2. The handstand is no longer performed with an arch. The body should be straight from the wrists to the toes. Body alignment is the most important consideration, and locked elbows are especially important. 3. Many girls will be unable to support their weight. Others will just not pay close attention to locking their elbows. The instructor must work with each one individually to be sure that the student can proceed safely. Those who are waiting to be checked by the instructor can assist by spotting those who are able to support themselves. 4. Have gymnasts experiment with the feeling of being upside down by kicking up to a near handstand and returning to a standing position.

| SKILL | DESCRIPTION | TEACHING TECHNIQUES AND OBSERVATION POINTS |

5. Keep head in line with body, eyes spotting hands.
6. Extend shoulders and hips. Do not allow shoulders to move ahead of hands.
7. Keep legs straight, abdomen pulled in, body tightened. Do not allow body to sag.

Spotting
1. Stand with one foot forward, one back in a stable stance. Arms should be up, ready to grasp thighs of gymnast.
2. Ask the gymnast to place her hands on either side of the spotter's forward foot.
3. Do not pull the gymnast up to the vertical position. Wait until she has succeeded in reaching the correct position on her own and then steady her and assist in helping her back to a stand.
4. Be prepared to keep her from overbalancing.
5. *Once she is able to kick to a handstand position with control,* help her to achieve a balanced position by checking to see that all body parts are aligned. Stand sideways where body alignment can best be seen, place hands on the gymnast's thighs, and pull up, stretching her body to its fullest extent. Use of two spotters is always safest.
6. Spotters must be reminded to watch their gymnast to be sure that elbows are locked and arms straight. Do not keep the gymnast in the inverted position for more than three to five seconds.
7. Assist the gymnast to come out of the inverted position by letting go of one leg and gently directing it back toward the floor.
8. It is not a good idea to practice this skill against a wall. It is too unyielding and a beginner's arms could give out, allowing a fall against the wall. This could cause injury to the head and neck.

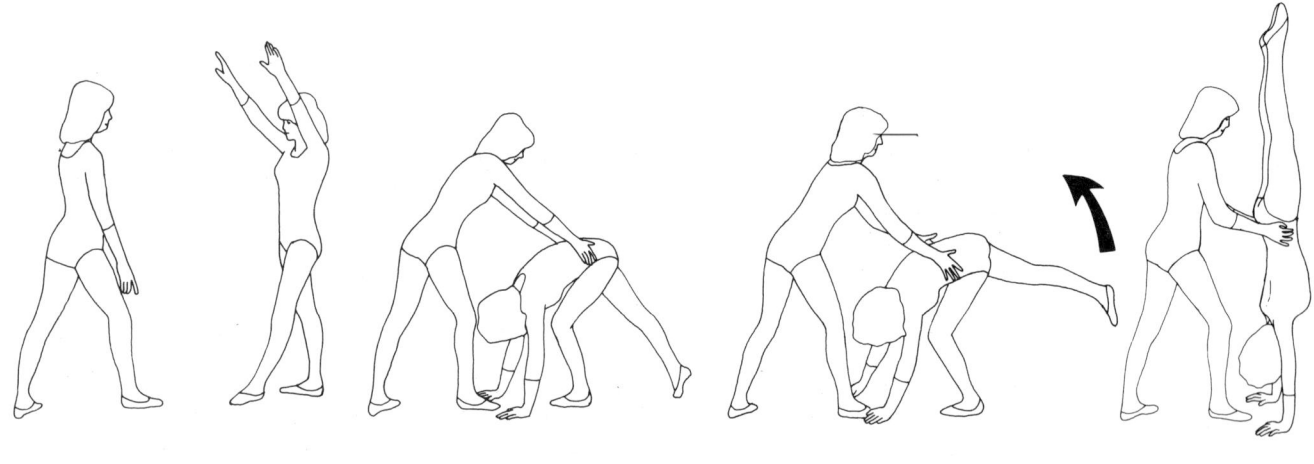

1   2   3   4

| SKILL | DESCRIPTION | TEACHING TECHNIQUES AND OBSERVATION POINTS |

Level II Skills

7. Forward Roll —Straddle

This is a difficult skill for most participants. It requires considerable hip flexibility to allow the weight to be shifted forward.
1. Begin in a straddle stand with the legs as wide apart as possible.
2. Reach forward onto the mat, placing the hands approximately shoulder width apart.
3. Follow through as in the forward roll-tuck, keeping the legs as wide apart as possible.
4. As the hips contact the floor, place the hands between the legs and push to raise the hips forward and upward.
5. Finish in a straddle stand.

1. Using the width of a mat, aim to keep the feet as close to the edge as possible, thus maintaining a wide straddle.
2. Have the students sit in a wide straddle and, placing the hands between the legs, as close to the body as possible, attempt to get up to a straddle stand.
3. Remind the students to use the momentum of the roll to their advantage.
4. This can also be performed from a stand (legs together) or from a straddle stand to a tuck position.

Spotting
1. A gentle lift on the hips or upper thighs can assist the gymnast.

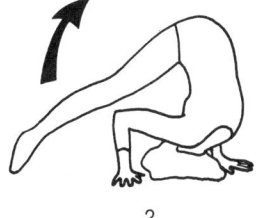
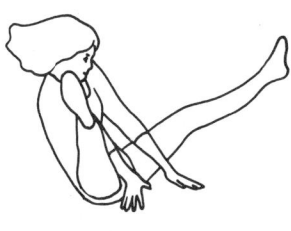

1   2   3

8. Handstand (3 seconds)

Review the Level I Handstand (with spotting).

1. The gymnast must be able to maintain a vertical handstand for three seconds. More important than the length of time it is held, is performing it with control (getting into and out of the inverted position) and achieving a vertical position.
2. Discuss with the gymnast possible methods of coming out of a handstand.
   a) Lifting one hand and turning off to one side.
   b) Overbalancing to a bridge.
   c) Stepping back down to a starting position.
   d) Forward roll (too difficult for this level).
3. Correct body alignment is essential.

Spotting
1. Until the gymnast can kick to a vertical and hold this position with assistance for five seconds, the spotting should be as described on page 26.
2. Later on the spotter can move to the side, grasp the leg, and assist in finding the balance position. From this angle incorrect body alignment can be seen more easily.

SKILL	DESCRIPTION	TEACHING TECHNIQUES AND OBSERVATION POINTS
9. Cartwheel	The gymnast must be able to perform a handstand before a correct cartwheel can be executed. The minimum requirement is that the gymnast is able to kick up to a vertical handstand position. 1. Begin the cartwheel as you would a handstand by raising the arms and the take-off leg. 2. Step into a "sideways" handstand by placing the hands at right angles to the take-off position. 3. The placement of the hands onto the mat is *not* simultaneous. The cartwheel is a four-count skill, 1-2-3-4; or hand, hand, foot, foot, all in a straight line. 4. The legs are in a straddle position, and as the performer passes through the inverted position the first leg is lowered to the mat, in line with the hands. 5. The upper body is then raised and the last leg is lowered to the mat in line with the first foot and about a shoulder width apart.	1. The arms should be beside the head throughout the skill, and legs should be straight. 2. The eyes watch the hands. The head should be slightly tilted up. 3. A chalk line drawn on the mat can be used to help the gymnast perform in a straight line. 4. A cartwheel quarter-turn is perhaps an easier variation of the cartwheel and lends itself better to a floor routine than the regular cartwheel. In the quarter-turn, lower the leg in line with the hands to assume a lunge position. The body should finish facing the starting position. 5. Additional variations include one-handed cartwheels, beat cartwheel (legs come together momentarily in the handstand position), cartwheel to splits. 6. Serious gymnasts should practice cartwheels on both sides. *Spotting* 1. Practice first spotting the gymnast in a straddle handstand from a sideways approach. 2. Determine first which hand the gymnast will place on the mat first. If it is right, stand about half a meter in front and slightly to the right of the gymnast. 3. Stand in a stable straddle stance to prepare for any overbalancing. 4. Keep head to the side to avoid legs hitting the face. 5. As in the regular handstand, allow and assist the gymnast to step down. 6. When the skill is performed in its entirety, the spotter places her hands on the gymnast's hips and follows through to a stable position.

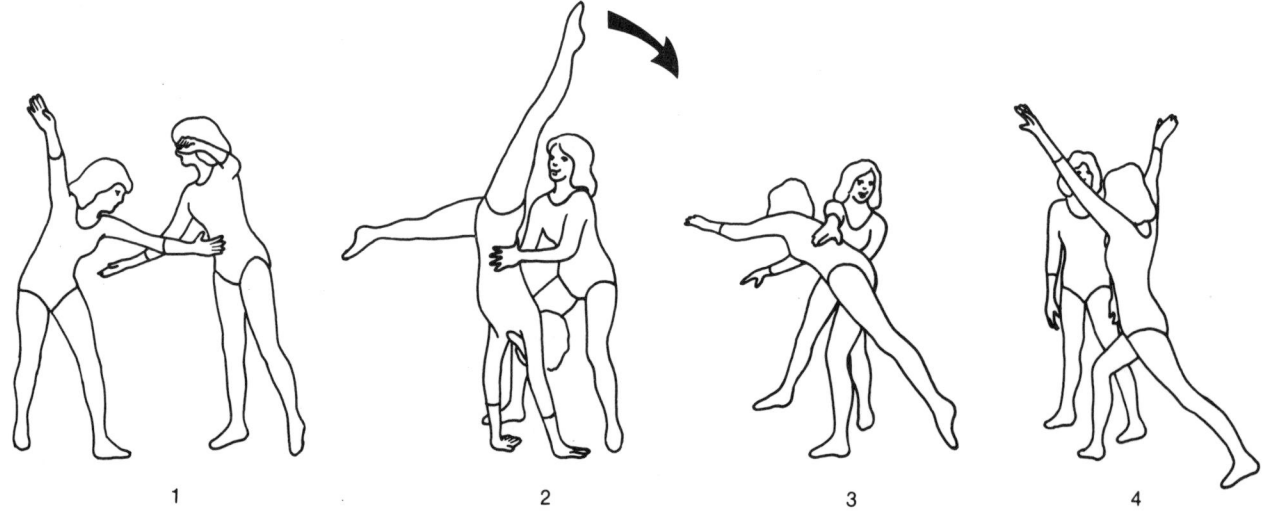

1 2 3 4

SKILL	DESCRIPTION	TEACHING TECHNIQUES AND OBSERVATION POINTS
10. Chassé	1. Step forward, bring feet together, step forward again with the same foot. "Step-together-step." The action is similar to the slide which is performed sideways. 2. Arms should be in second position (see Basic Ballet Positions, page 18) or sideways. 3. With weight on the left foot and the knee bent slightly, step forward on the right foot, bending at the knee (demi-plié). 4. Spring off the floor and bring the left leg to contact the back of the right leg. Land on the left foot, then step again on the right foot.	1. Attempt to spring as high as possible and point the foot toward the floor while in the air. 2. Do not allow arms to waver. Hold in second position. 
11. Waltz Step	1. The waltz step is a combination of three walking steps. It can be thought of as a "down-up-up" step. 2. The first step is a long step performed with a plié (bent knee). The second and third steps are two short steps usually done on the toes. 3. Arms are held in second position.	1. This step may be performed backward or in a curve, as well as forward. 2. The two "up" steps can also be used to perform a turn. 3. The arms can remain in second or be lowered on the "down" step and raised for the two "up" steps. 
12. Arabesque Hop	1. The arabesque hop is initiated in the same way as the chassé, only the left leg is raised upward and backward while a hop is executed on the right leg. 2. Arms are best held up in a "V" position above the head, palms down.	1. Keep the upper body in an upright position. Do not allow the body to bend forward as the leg is raised at the back. 2. After jumping up, the legs should be straight and the feet extended. 3. This is an easy dance move to try after a forward roll. It is a good mass tumbling skill.

SKILL	DESCRIPTION	TEACHING TECHNIQUES AND OBSERVATION POINTS
13. Body Wave	1. Assume a bent knee position, with legs together, head down, and arms forward and down. 2. As the knees slowly straighten, the hips come forward and the back is arched. Keep shoulders and head well back. 3. The arms move downward, backward and upward with the body. 4. Finish high on toes.	1. The backward position of the head and shoulders is essential. 2. Think of a wave moving through the body starting at the knees, flowing to the hips, then to the shoulders. 3. This is a difficult skill.

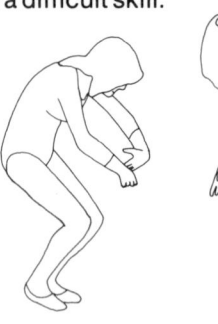  

1   2   3

14. Turns on One Foot	1. Stand with weight on left foot, right leg extended forward. 2. Step onto right foot and, leading with head, turn body to right to face opposite direction. 3. Left leg should be the last part of the body to complete the half turn. The left foot finishes in front of the right, extended forward. 4. Arms can be in a "V" overhead or begin to the left and swing across the body and overhead, thus giving momentum to the turn.	1. The turn is executed high on the ball of the foot. 2. Body alignment is essential. Head is held up and shoulders relaxed. 3. Allow performers to be creative in their leg and arm positions—they could use straight leg or bent knee, for instance. 4. A full turn may be executed by rotating around to original position.

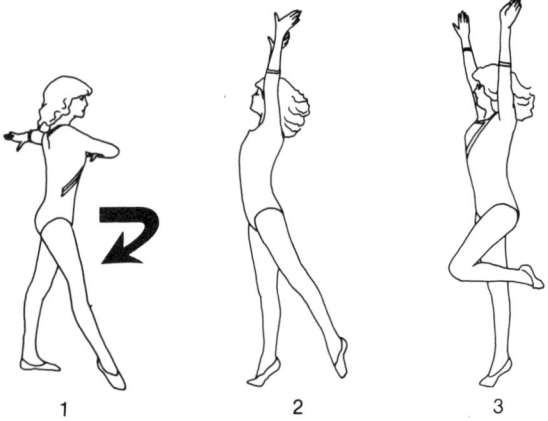

1   2   3

Level III Skills

15. Headspring on a Rolled Mat	This skill will be broken down into three sections. The gymnast must master each section in turn before moving on.	1. Do not allow the gymnast to practice the third part of the skill until she can perform a controlled overbalanced inverted pike. 2. It is important for each gymnast to "feel" the overbalanced position and know that this is the point at which the legs must be whipped over. 3. Timing is crucial in this skill. It is better to be a little late in whipping the legs than too early. The instructor may wish to use a verbal cue such as "Now!" to assist the gymnast in finding the correct point at which to whip the legs over.

1   2

SKILL	DESCRIPTION	TEACHING TECHNIQUES AND OBSERVATION POINTS

1. Place the hands shoulder width apart on the rolled mat. Place the forehead on the mat in line with the hands. Jump to an inverted pike position keeping the "toes by the nose" and legs straight. Do not allow the neck to roll, and keep the back straight.
2. After the gymnast has mastered the correct inverted pike position, the spotter then allows the gymnast to experience the "overbalanced" position. The hips are allowed to overbalance while the legs remain straight and toes close to the nose.
3. In mastering the third section, the gymnast jumps to the inverted pike position, slowly overbalances and then whips the *straight* legs over to a standing position on the opposite side of the mat. The arms extend forcefully as the hips move over.

Spotting
1. When the gymnast attempts the first section of this skill, the spotter stands on the opposite side of the rolled mat from the gymnast, feet apart, one foot in front of the other. The spotter grasps the gymnast's hips as she jumps into the inverted pike position and steadies her.
2. In the second section, the spotter lowers the gymnast's hips to correct the overbalanced position, then returns her to the original inverted pike position.
3. When the gymnast attempts the complete skill *two* spotters, one on either side of the gymnast, are necessary. They should kneel on the opposite side of the mat from the gymnast. The hand closest to the gymnast is placed on her wrist and the second hand on her hips. Spotters follow the gymnast to a stand by extending their arms. They should hold onto the gymnast until a controlled standing position is reached.

1   2   3   4

16. Handstand to Forward Roll

1. From a controlled handstand position, slightly overbalance.
2. Bend arms slowly, flex hips slowly, go into a pike position.

1. Timing is important—some gymnasts may have a tendency to tuck the head too soon (before they have overbalanced). This will result in all the weight coming down on the neck. If they tuck the head too late or overbalance too much, they will land heavily on the back.

SKILL	DESCRIPTION	TEACHING TECHNIQUES AND OBSERVATION POINTS

| | 3. Tuck head under, place shoulders on the mat, roll forward, and come to a stand. | 2. This is a good time to introduce the handstand snap down. If a vertical held position is not quite reached and the gymnast comes down from the handstand to her original position, forcefully snap the legs down from the hips, at the same time pushing hard with the hands to a standing position. A high rebound jump should follow this skill. Spotters should stand to the side, hands on the gymnast's waist, and lift her hips to assist with the push off. |

Spotting
1. Two spotters, one on either side, should grasp the gymnast's legs and gently lower them as she initiates and completes the roll.
2. Begin with lots of spotting until you can feel that the gymnast has control and her timing is correct. Then gradually ease off on the spotting.

17. Backward Roll to Extension (Handstand)

1. Proceed as for the backward roll with legs straight and hands placed on mat under shoulders. As the hips come over the chest, forcefully thrust the legs upward, at the same time pushing with the hands and extending the arms.
2. Lift the head and come to a momentary handstand. Step down one leg at a time to stand, or snap down as in a round-off.

1. Timing is again crucial in this skill. Spotters are particularly helpful in assisting the gymnast to find the correct time to thrust legs vertically and extend arms.

Spotting
1. Use two spotters, one on either side, slightly ahead of the gymnast (where her head would be if a backward roll were executed).
2. As the hips come over the chest, grasp the legs above the knee and lift to the handstand position.

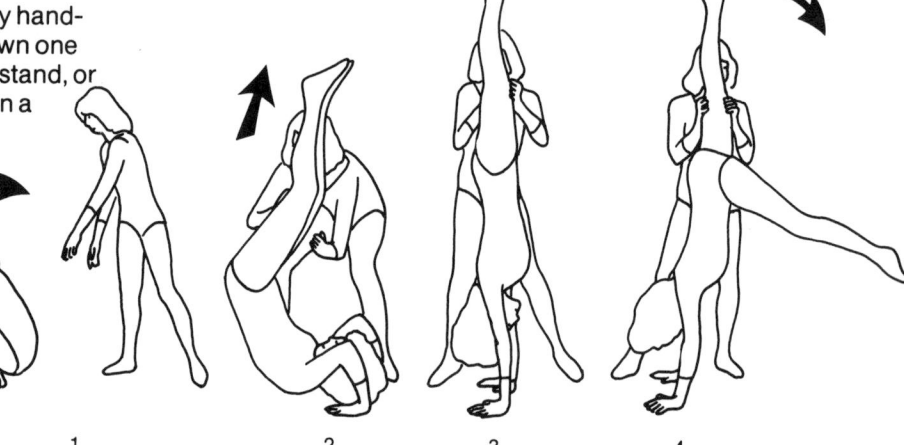

18. Cartwheel Series

1. A Cartwheel Series involves two or more cartwheels done without a pause in between.

1. Arms must be kept close to the head throughout so there is no pause while they catch up with the body.
2. A variety of different cartwheels can be used.
3. The cartwheels need not be performed quickly to avoid a pause—just evenly.

Spotting
1. As for cartwheel.
2. Move with gymnast for the second cartwheel.

SKILL	DESCRIPTION	TEACHING TECHNIQUES AND OBSERVATION POINTS

19. Round-off

Gymnasts should be able to perform a cartwheel and a handstand snap down before attempting this skill. The primary purpose of the round-off is to change forward momentum to backward momentum.

1. Begin with a hurdle, a step-hop preceded by running steps. There are two main styles—one where the legs are both extended downward, and the other where one leg is bent. Arms and chest are raised up in both methods.
2. From a hurdle the hands are placed on the mat, as in the cartwheel.
3. As the body reaches the inverted position the legs come together to the handstand position.
4. As the body completes the half-turn and overbalances, push hard with the hands and shoulders. The hips are vigorously flexed and the upper body is lifted.
5. As the feet contact the mat, immediately rebound and lift the arms vertically upward.

1. Have the performer practice the round-off first in slow motion to get the feeling of bringing the legs together and turning before snapping the legs down. From the very beginning have the students rebound with a high jump.
2. The gymnast then progresses to the round-off with hurdle.
3. Be sure to remind performers to place hands on mat in direct line with body. The hands must push off the mat and the shoulders extend. The chest and head should be raised as the feet snap down. Legs must remain straight.

    If hand placement is incorrect, have the gymnast put chalk on her hands, then perform the round-off. An imprint of her hands will remain, and her error can be pointed out more easily.

Spotting
1. When the gymnast places her hands in preparation for the round-off in slow motion, the spotter should be facing her back, placing hands on the gymnast's hips, and twisting the hips away. Gently push toward direction of landing.
2. When performing from a hurdle, the spotter stands to the non-turning side and grasps the hip area.

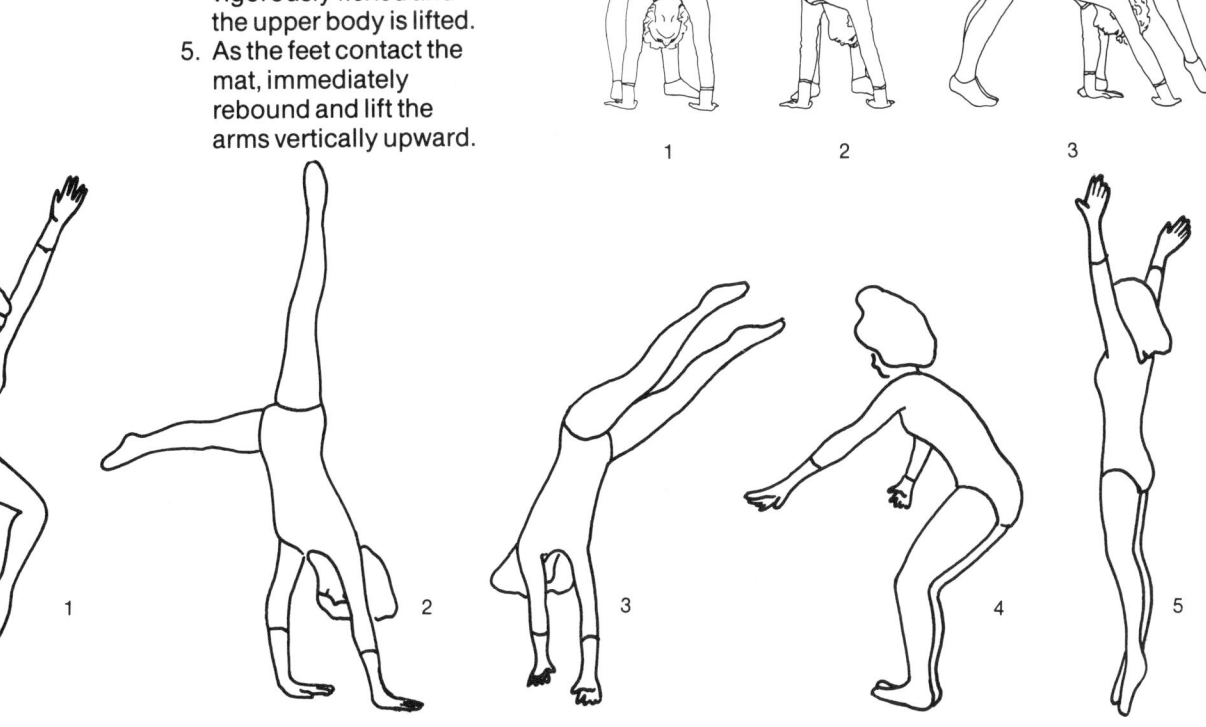

| SKILL | DESCRIPTION | TEACHING TECHNIQUES AND OBSERVATION POINTS |

20. Round-off Backward Roll to a Knee Scale

1. As the gymnast contacts the mat with her feet at the completion of the round-off, the knees bend and the backward roll is performed.
2. As the legs come over the head one leg is extended and the other bent at the knee to form a base of support. The gymnast finishes in a knee scale.

1. Many of the skills that follow a dynamic round-off are very advanced and beyond the capabilities of the average class participant. The backward roll, however, can easily be combined with a slow, well-controlled round-off.
2. Be sure to get the hands backward and under the shoulders for the backward roll.

Spotting

1. The spotting is the same as for the round-off and the backward roll.

1 2 3 4

21. Split Leap

1. A leap involves a transfer of weight from one foot to the other, and involves height and distance. As the transfer of weight is made, the body is completely suspended in the air. A correctly performed leap is a very explosive movement.
2. After the back leg initiates the forward and upward movement of the body the front leg extends forward as the back leg reaches backward and upward to an even split position. The head and chest are held high. The arms are usually held in opposition to the legs.

1. To assist the gymnast to experience the correct position of the split leap, it is helpful to have two spotters, one on either side, lift the gymnast by the arms as she leaps. This gives her the height and time to split the legs properly.
2. It is helpful to precede the leap with a chassé or step-together.

SKILL	DESCRIPTION	TEACHING TECHNIQUES AND OBSERVATION POINTS
22. Sissone	A sissone can be performed either forward or backward. The sissone described here is performed forward. 1. Begin the movement with the legs in fifth position (see page 19) with the right foot in front. 2. Bend both knees and spring diagonally forward on the right foot while the left leg is raised at the back. Land on the right foot and lower the left foot to fifth position, knees bent.	1. It is perhaps easiest to step through this skill first. Step forward on the right foot, bringing the left foot behind the right. 2. Then bend both knees and spring forward, following through as described. 3. Arm position is best left optional. The right arm can be held at the side and the left arm forward. 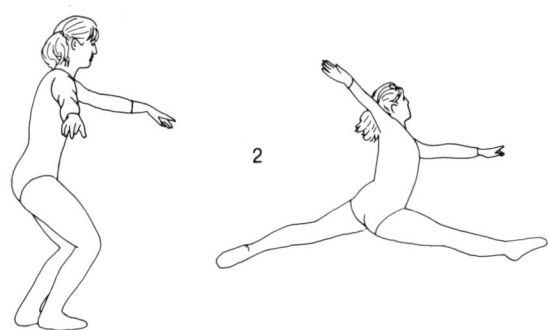
23. Tour Jêté	1. Step on the left foot; this is most easily performed using the momentum from sliding steps as in the Level III Routine (see below). 2. Kick the left leg forward and upward. 3. Twist the body quickly 180° and land on the right foot. 4. Swing the left leg to the rear to hold a lunge position.	1. Have the students perform this skill on a line. This will help them get into the correct body positions. 2. Hold the head up and do not allow the shoulders to lean forward or backward. 3. If the gymnasts can concentrate on swinging the arms overhead as the left leg swings forward, this will give their Tour Jêté added height. 
24. Routine  Step Kick	1. Sissone (right foot leading) 2. Sissone (left foot leading) 3. Run four steps 4. Cartwheel quarter-turn 5. Three back steps to corner 6. Stretch on toes 7. Bent knee pose 8. Quarter-turn to right	1. The Level III routine incorporates skills from the previous two levels as well as some taught in the Level III unit. The gymnasts learn to perform a specific set of skills and to perform them in such a way that the routine flows from one element to the next. The routine involves dance movements as well as tumbling elements. 2. This routine can be performed on the floor with mats strategically placed for protection during the tumbling elements, notably the forward roll and the round-off backward roll. 3. It is best for all arm positions to be optional with suggestions and guidance coming from the instructor.

SKILL	DESCRIPTION	TEACHING TECHNIQUES AND OBSERVATION POINTS

Front Scale

Pose

9. Step kick (on right foot—raise left foot)
10. Step kick (on left foot—raise right foot)
11. Scissors jump
12. Quarter-turn right (to face starting position)
13. Two sliding steps to the right
14. Tour jêté to lunge position
15. Step forward, full turn on one foot
16. Front scale
17. Forward roll to stand
18. Run
19. Round-off
20. Back roll to knee scale
21. Pose or balance (optional position)

4. To assist the performers, mark the area off with cones and draw arrows on the floor indicating the direction they are to follow.
5. If there is a Level IV gymnast available, it is helpful if she demonstrates the routine in its entirety. If this is not possible, break it down into *three* lines and present it in that manner.
6. Stress form, grace and poise. Be sure the gymnasts realize that the routine must be memorized.
7. Level IV gymnasts are encouraged to make up their own routines.

Scissors Jump

1   2

Level IV Skills

25. Headspring

Please refer to the headspring on a rolled mat described on pages 30 and 31 (Level III).

1. Gradually reduce the height of the rolled mat, allowing the gymnast to get used to whipping the legs over as quickly as possible.
2. If the skill was properly learned on a rolled mat, performing it on the floor will not be difficult. Be sure to review and observe each gymnast's headspring on a rolled mat before attempting to teach the skill on the floor.

Spotting
As described for headspring on a rolled mat.

26. One-armed Cartwheel

This is a variation of the cartwheel described on page 28.

1. The gymnast must be able to perform a cartwheel.
2. It is strictly preference as to which arm is used for support.

  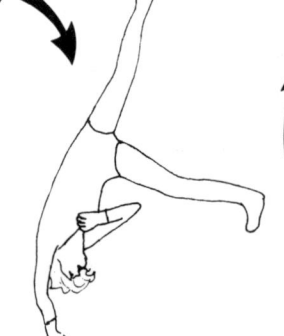 

1   2   3   4

SKILL	DESCRIPTION	TEACHING TECHNIQUES AND OBSERVATION POINTS

It may be performed using the "near" arm or the "far" arm. The near arm would normally be placed down first, and the far arm would normally be placed on the mat second. In either case, the free arm is placed alongside the body while the skill is performed.

Spotting
The same as for the Cartwheel.

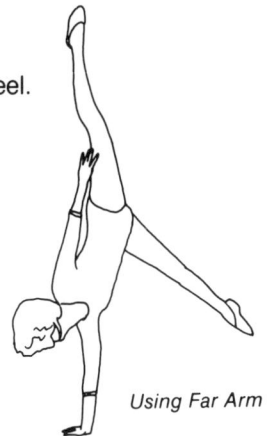

Using Far Arm

27. Front Walkover

a) Front limber

The lead-up to a front walkover is the front limber. Although the limber by itself is rarely used in gymnastics, it is the basic movement in many other skills, especially the walkover "family."
1. Stretch the arms above the head and raise one leg as for preparation for a handstand.
2. Kick to a momentary handstand, and *as balance is lost,* arch back and move legs in an arc to place feet on the mat.
3. Just as feet touch the mat, push with hands and push hips forward over feet and extend legs to stand.

1. For many gymnasts the correct performance of this skill will be impossible due to poor shoulder and back flexibility. If the performer is unable to achieve a full backbend or bridge position, do not have her perform a limber. Instead, have her work on the backbend and/or assist in spotting.
2. The position of the arms and the head is also extremely important. The head and arms must be kept back at all times. If the head or arms are brought forward, the arch is lost, and the distribution of weight is changed so the body will collapse into a sitting position. Arms must be kept straight.

Spotting
1. Initially two spotters should be used, one on either side of the gymnast. Depending on the height of the gymnast, spotting may be done kneeling or standing.
2. As the performer places her hands on the floor, grasp the upper arm (palm up and thumb outside of arm) with the hand nearest the gymnast.
3. As the body arches place the remaining hand on the upper back and assist the gymnast to a stand.

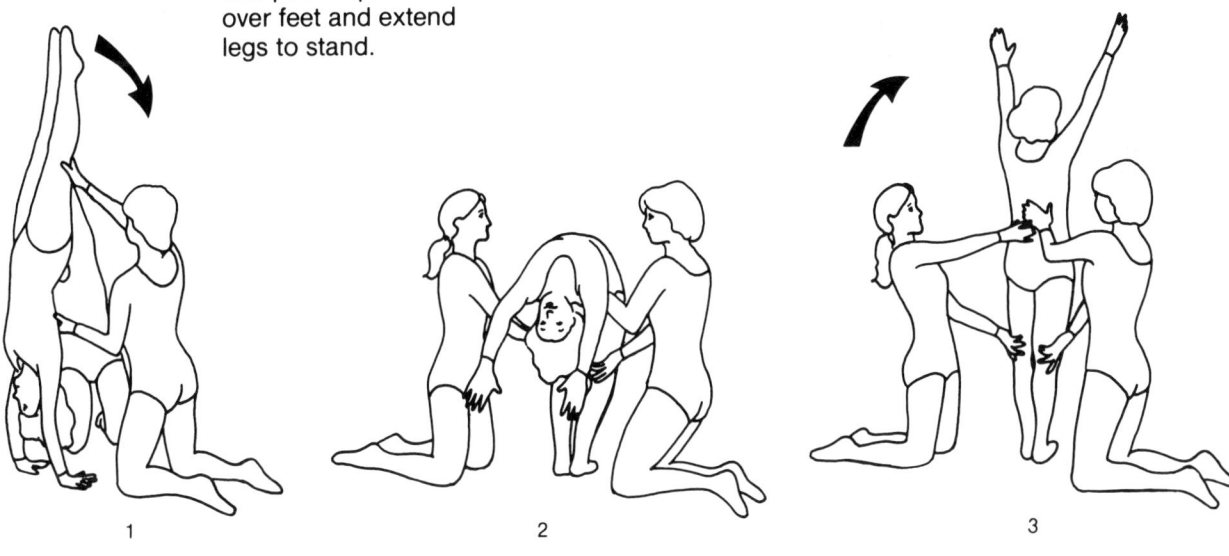

SKILL	DESCRIPTION	TEACHING TECHNIQUES AND OBSERVATION POINTS
b) Front walkover	1. The walkover is much like the limber only the legs are kept in a split throughout. 2. Stretch and prepare for the walkover as you would a handstand. 3. Step forward on one foot, place hands on floor while lifting the remaining foot up through a handstand, and arch the back over until this lead foot touches the ground.	1. In order to keep the head well back and between the arms, place something on the mat for the gymnast to look at. 2. The ideal walkover shows a split of the legs in the inverted position and the last leg down is held up as high as possible. 3. Legs must be straight throughout. 4. This is a difficult skill to master. The timing of the thrust of the hips and push of the hands is crucial. *Spotting* As for the limber.

1 2 3 4 5

	4. Push the hips forward, shifting the weight forward, and push the hands off the mat. 5. Lower the remaining foot to the ground and raise the head and arms to an upright position.	
28. Back Walkover	Before performing this element be sure the gymnast is able to bend backward and place her hands on the mat, supporting her weight without her elbows collapsing.	1. Back and shoulder flexibility are very important in this skill. 2. The stretch at the beginning of the skill with the weight on one foot is crucial. 3. Legs must be straight throughout. 4. Timing is all important. If the lead leg is brought over too soon, there will be a slight hop as the hands hit the mat. If the lead leg is too late, there will be a pause and much of the performance will be done by the spotters! If the timing is correct, the skill will be smooth and flowing.

SKILL	DESCRIPTION	TEACHING TECHNIQUES AND OBSERVATION POINTS
	1. Have the gymnast prepare for the back walkover by putting her weight on one foot while placing the *toes* of the other foot on the mat a few inches in front of the support leg. Both legs must remain straight. 2. Stretch the body upward, arms by the ears and straight. As the head drops backward, the arms follow reaching for the mat. 3. Just as the hands touch the mat the lead leg is lifted vigorously upward and over. The support leg then immediately pushes off the mat to allow the gymnast to reach a split position with her legs, while in the inverted position. 4. As the lead foot touches the mat, the hands push off, the chest is raised, and the last leg is held up in an arabesque.	*Spotting* 1. Begin with two spotters, one on either side of the performer. With the near hand, one spotter lifts the gymnast's lead leg, while the other spotter assists with the support leg. The far hand supports the upper back as the gymnast lowers her hands to the mat. 2. The spotters may assist the gymnast in the correct timing of this element by initiating the leg lift at the appropriate time. If there is only one spotter, she should stand on the gymnast's leg side.

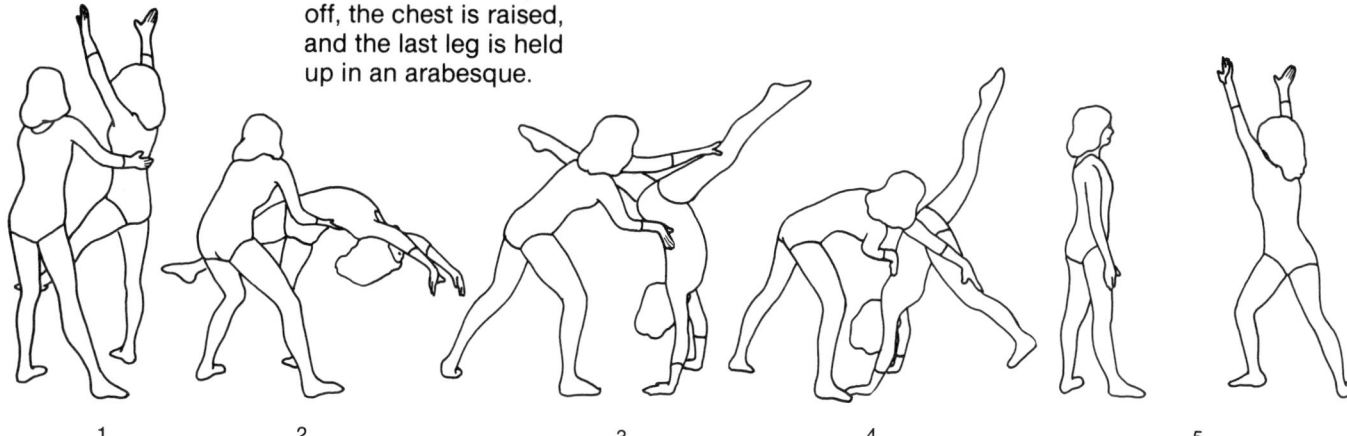

1   2   3   4   5

| **29. Back and Front Walkovers in Series** | Walkovers performed in a series must be done without a pause or any steps taken in between elements. The performance must be smooth and flowing. | 1. To perform walkovers in a series it is suggested that gymnasts be able to execute a walkover without spotting.
2. To perform front walkovers in a series the gymnast must be prepared to hold the last leg up ready to step immediately into the next walkover.
Spotting
The spotting is the same as for walkovers, although the spotters must be prepared to move with the gymnast on to the next walkover. |

SKILL	DESCRIPTION	TEACHING TECHNIQUES AND OBSERVATION POINTS
30. Handspring	1. Using a hurdle (see description under Round-off, page 33), plant the take-off foot and reach outward with straight arms. With a strong kick, lift the remaining leg upward and over, while at the same time pushing off with the take-off foot. 2. Push up with the hands so there is a total body lift and the body is suspended momentarily in the air. 3. The legs come together as the body passes through the handstand position. Reach for the mat with the toes. 4. Body is slightly arched upon landing, arms by the ears, head back. Knees flexed to absorb weight on landing.	1. The push from the legs should be emphasized as this action is mainly responsible for inverting and rotating the body. 2. If the thrust of the legs starts just before the hands contact the mat the body will invert faster and the "pop" action will be more dynamic. 3. Reach long and low with the hands. 4. Have the gymnasts practice kicking forcefully to a handstand. 5. Gymnasts should attempt to learn this from a short approach, thus putting emphasis on explosive leg power. *Spotting* 1. As for the limber. It is best to use two spotters in the initial stages. Spotters must position themselves so they can support the gymnast adequately. 2. It is helpful to practice the hurdle and hand placement without following through with the entire skill, so that the spotters can make necessary adjustments without risk to the gymnast.

1 2 3 4

31. Handspring Walkout	1. This skill is a variation of the handspring, and therefore the entire body must be momentarily suspended in the air.	1. Same as for handspring. 2. The legs must be kept in a wide stride position.

SKILL	DESCRIPTION	TEACHING TECHNIQUES AND OBSERVATION POINTS

2. The legs are kept in a stride position throughout as in the walkover. It is not, however, a running walkover.
3. There must be a strong push from both feet and from the hands so that the lead leg contacts the mat almost straight.
4. The hips should be forward.

Spotting
Same as for handspring.

32. Valdez

This skill can be thought of as a back walkover from a sitting position.
1. Begin by sitting on the floor with both legs extended forward and together. Bend the left knee, placing the foot flat on the floor. The right leg remains extended.
2. The left hand is placed on the floor behind the hips. The arm should be straight.
3. The right arm is extended parallel to the right leg.
4. Thrust the right arm overhead, onto the floor, at the same time extend the left leg.
5. Kick the right leg upward to push the body to an inverted position. The left hand will rotate around and the right will be placed on the floor, shoulder width apart from the right.
6. Complete the back walkover from the inverted position.

1. Have the gymnast practice pushing up to a backbend from the starting position of the valdez.
2. Repeat this movement raising the right leg as high as possible. Then do the entire element in one movement.
3. The hips must be thrust upward as the bent leg is extended.
4. Do not allow the arms to bend.
5. Keep legs straight.
6. Some gymnasts may find it easier to perform this skill with the forward arm on the same side as the bent knee.
7. Have the gymnast follow the fingers of the forward arm with her eyes as the arm moves overhead. This helps to get the head in the correct position and initiates the arch in the back.
8. Do not have the bent knee too close to the chest or too far away from it. It must be placed at a reasonable distance so the gymnast can get into an arched position.

Spotting
1. Kneel on the left side (the bent knee side) and place one hand under the upper thigh and the other hand on the upper back. Assist the gymnast to the arched position, at the same time directing the hips backward.
2. Be prepared for a loss of balance on the part of the gymnast should she be unable to get the free arm around and down on the mat.

| SKILL | DESCRIPTION | TEACHING TECHNIQUES AND OBSERVATION POINTS |

33. Back Handspring

This is an advanced skill, and the time and attention it requires for safety reasons make it more appropriate for the advanced gymnast or the gymnast who works outside of the classroom. The description of this skill includes descriptions of several lead-up activities. It is best to have two spotters at all times when gymnasts are performing these lead-ups, both for safety reasons and to ensure that techniques are correct.

a) Back Handspring Lead-up

1. Begin with both feet together, arms by the ears.
2. Drop the head back, arms follow to perform a slow back limber. Arms are straight throughout.
3. As the hands touch the mat and the body passes through the handstand position, the legs are snapped down and the hands push off the mat, the head and upper body lift to a stand.
4. Repeat this several times, getting faster as the gymnast becomes comfortable with the movement.
5. Practice the snap down from the handstand position. Spotters may provide additional lift by lifting up on the hips as the gymnast snaps down.
6. Have the gymnast get used to the idea of jumping at the end of the back handspring. Practice jumping after the handstand snap down and the back limber.

Spotting
1. It is best to have two spotters at all times.
2. Kneel on the mat, one arm on her back, the other on the back of her upper thigh.
3. Lift the gymnast slowly through the back limber, helping to get the gymnast oriented to the idea of falling backwards.
4. Be sure to support the gymnast throughout the entire movement, especially when her hands contact the mat. Be sure the gymnast's arms are straight to support her weight.
5. This is a slow, graceful movement.

b) Back Handspring

1. Stand with the feet slightly apart and parallel. Arms forward and horizontal.

1. The gymnast should understand the importance of extending all flexed body parts in the starting position. This action must be vigorous and powerful.

SKILL	DESCRIPTION	TEACHING TECHNIQUES AND OBSERVATION POINTS

2. Swing the arms downward and bend the knees as if sitting on a chair. Shoulders should be kept back.
3. Swing the arms overhead vigorously and thrust the head backward. Push off the mat by straightening the ankle, knee and hip joints. The body is extended during the flight.
4. Arms are straight as they touch the mat and the body passes through the handstand position. From this position the legs are snapped down, the head and chest lifted, and the finish is a standing position.

2. Keep the shoulders over the hips when "sitting down on the chair."
3. Do not allow the hips to be flexed too soon. The handstand position must be reached.
4. Legs should be together after the take off.
5. There should be an even rhythm to the sound of first the hands and then the feet hitting the floor.
6. Have the gymnast perform a high jumping motion after she has completed her back handspring. This should be automatic.
7. Remind the gymnast she is driving *up* and *back*.

c) Variation
   Back Handspring
   Step-out

As the body passes through the handstand part of the back handspring, one leg is lowered before the other, as in the back walkover. This is a much more feminine movement.

34. Round-off Back Handspring

1. In performing the round-off the gymnast must snap the feet down as close as possible to the hands. This puts the body in an off-balance position moving backwards.
2. The back handspring is performed immediately without pause.

1. This is an advanced combination of skills and while one may be able to perform both with confidence, putting them together for the first time can be difficult for the gymnast.
2. The gymnast must be able to perform both skills very well before attempting to do them together.
3. Practice this combination in slow motion to begin with. Mark out on the mat where the hand placement for the round-off will be, and exactly where the gymnast will perform the back handspring.
4. Have the gymnast pause before she initiates her back handspring. This allows the gymnast to orientate herself and the spotters to ready themselves.
5. As the timing is perfected, shorten the pause, thus making good use of the momentum from the round-off.
6. The round-off is often called a short round-off, as opposed to a long round-off which causes the body to go upward.

SKILL	DESCRIPTION	TEACHING TECHNIQUES AND OBSERVATION POINTS

35. Optional Routine

Design a routine using skills appropriate to the gymnast's ability. The length, and the use of music, is optional.

1. When designing a floor routine, one must consider the following:
   a) Utilize the full space.
   b) Perform at a variety of levels i.e., high, low.
   c) Include changes in rhythm.
   d) Include turns, leaps, and jumps.
   e) Include poses and balances.
   f) Stress individuality and creativity.
   g) Distribute tumbling skills throughout the routine.
   h) Do not repeat skills.
2. Some students may have difficulty getting their routines started. Allow them to use the Level III routine and change the various skills to ones more appropriate to their ability or preference.
3. Have the students practice their judging on each other's routines.

B. Uneven Parallel Bars

Strength is a primary consideration in the performance of this spectacular event. Properly performed, a routine on the uneven parallel bars is a combination of swing movements around both the high and the low bars, and movements from one bar to the other. This requires strength in the arms, shoulders, abdomen and back areas. These are particularly weak areas for most girls, so only those skills that are considered within the capabilities of the average girl of secondary school age have been included in this handbook.

Many of the movements are "orientation moves," serving to familiarize the students with the bars. They involve inverted positions, movement to the high bar, and positions where the student may try to support herself. Many of the skills do not have specific names, so a "descriptive name" has been used.

Instructors may find many girls fearful of working on the high bar. In beginning levels, do not force movement to the high bar except for the long hang position. In most cases, girls who can hang from their hands for at least ten seconds will not find this apparatus difficult.

Uneven bars should be introduced after the tumbling, as they seem to have a tremendous drawing effect on the girls.

General Safety

1. It is important to check the apparatus before each session to see that all supports, cables, and locks are securely fastened.
2. If the equipment has to be transported from a storage area, care must be taken in moving it from one place to another. The equipment is heavy and should be handled in a controlled manner. Feet must be kept clear when moving the apparatus and when the bars are being lowered into place on the floor.
3. When the bars have been raised or lowered, the locking devices should be checked to see they are secure. Care should be taken in lowering and raising the bars. If it is done incorrectly, the bar may suddenly slip and injure someone.
4. Mats should be placed under and around the bars. A double thickness of mats should be provided for dismounts.
5. If a beat board is used for mounts, it should be removed as soon as the gymnast is safely on the bar. A fall onto the beat board from the bars could be very serious.
6. The use of magnesium chalk on the hands helps prevent the hands from slipping. Do not allow chalk to build up on the bars. A fine piece of sandpaper will remove excess chalk and keep the bars in good condition.
7. One person only on the bars at a time should be the general rule. However some of the lead-up activities may allow two at one time, if there is close supervision.
8. The bars should be carefully positioned so there is adequate room for mounts and dismounts.

SKILL	DESCRIPTION	TEACHING TECHNIQUES AND OBSERVATION POINTS

9. There are four basic grips.
   a) *Forward or Regular Grip*—hands are over the bar with the back of the hand facing upward. This grip is used for most of the uneven bar skills. Position of thumbs is optional.
   b) *Reverse Grip*—hands are behind or under the bar with the thumb around the bar.
   c) *Mixed Grip*—one hand in forward grip, one hand in reverse grip.
   d) *Eagle Grip*—with her back to the bar, the gymnast reaches backward to form a "V," grasping the bar in a regular grip.

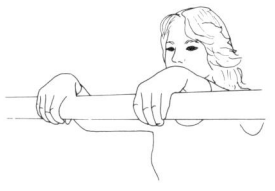 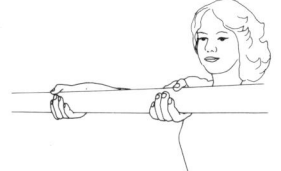  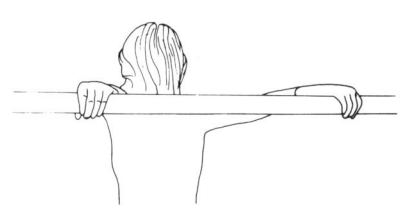

a *Forward Grip*   b *Reverse Grip*   c *Mixed Grip*   d *Eagle Grip*

Level I Skills

1. Long Hang

1. Stand behind the high bar facing the low bar. Jump up and grasp the high bar with both hands, using a regular grip.
2. Arms are straight, head between arms.
3. Legs together, body tight and firm.

1. This is a very easy skill for students to perform. Stress good form and check for body tightness.
2. Many students will be unable to reach the high bar on their own, so assistance from a spotter will be needed.

Spotting
1. Stand behind the gymnast, hands grasping the waist. On a count of three, lift the gymnast to the high bar while she jumps.
2. Steady her in position.

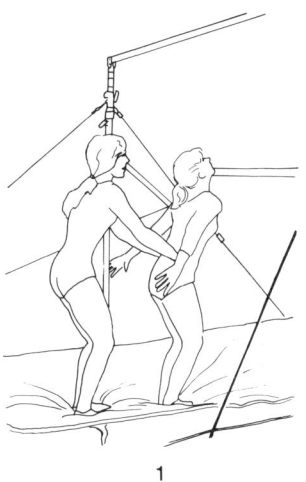 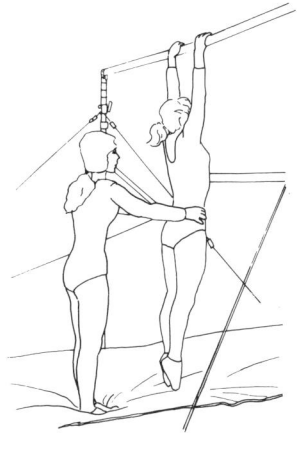

1 2

SKILL	DESCRIPTION	TEACHING TECHNIQUES AND OBSERVATION POINTS
2. Front Support Mount (Low Bar)	1. Face the low bar, hands shoulder width apart on the low bar. Hands regular grip. 2. Bend the knees and jump up so the arms are straight and the upper thigh is resting on the low bar. Shoulders are forward of the bar. 3. The body is tight and in line.	1. The shoulders should not be hunched. They must be extended and the head held up. 2. The body should be tight and slightly arched. 3. Some overweight girls will be unable to do this without spotting. *Spotting* 1. Stand to the side of the gymnast and grasp her upper thigh. 2. On a count of three, lift the gymnast to the bar as she jumps. 3. Steady her into position.

1

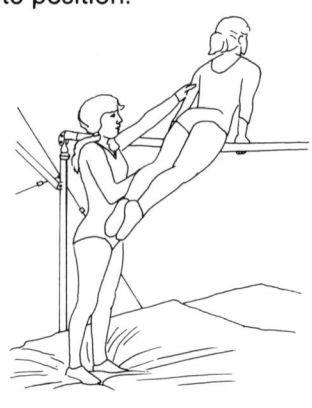
2

3. Rear Dismount	1. From the front support position, bend at the hips, allowing the legs to swing under the bar. 2. As the legs swing back, lift the hips away from the bar and push with the arms. 3. Swing upward and away from the low bar to a stand.	1. Do not allow the arms to bend as the hips come away from the bar. 2. Push the bar away with the arms. *Spotting* 1. Stand beside the gymnast, on the same side of the bar that she is on. 2. Grasp her wrist with one hand and place your hand on her upper thigh, palm up.

1

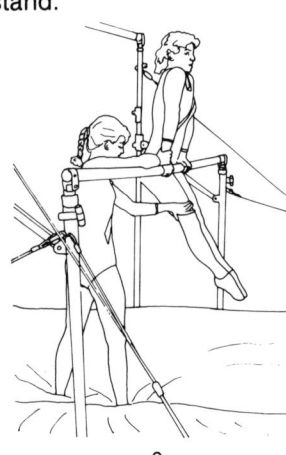
2

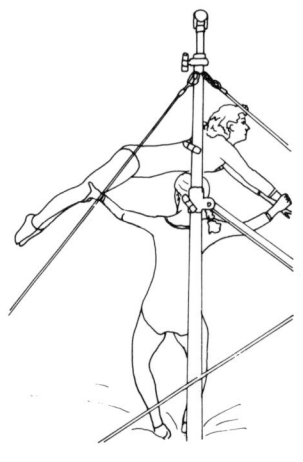
3

4

SKILL	DESCRIPTION	TEACHING TECHNIQUES AND OBSERVATION POINTS
		3. As she bends at the hips, allow your hand to move with the thigh and then lift up as the legs come back and away from the bar. 4. Move with the gymnast to a standing position, holding the wrist until the gymnast is under control.
4. Straddle Over Low Bar to Stand	1. Jump to long hang on the high bar. Straddle the legs, swinging them up and over the low bar. 2. Bring the legs together so the backs of the thighs are resting on the low bar. Slide forward and sit on the low bar momentarily. Simultaneously release the high bar with hands. 3. Jump off the low bar to stand. Legs are straight throughout.	1. This combination of skills is an "orientation" skill, to get the gymnasts used to moving from one bar to the other. 2. Some gymnasts will not have the strength to raise their legs over the low bar in the straddle position. If this is the case, spotting will be necessary. 3. initially, do not allow the gymnasts to jump from the low bar without a spotter. Gymnasts must continue to hold the high bar until the spotter has moved into an assist position for landing. 4. Hold the landing to show control. *Spotting* 1. Spot the long hang as described previously. 2. From behind the gymnast, place hands on backs of her thighs, straddle her legs and lift them over the low bar, being careful not to catch hands between bar and gymnast. 3. Spotter now moves to the far side of the low bar where the gymnast will land. 4. Reach up over the low bar to grasp the gymnast's waist. On signal the gymnast lets go of the high bar, jumps off the low bar, and lands on the mat. Spotter steadies the gymnast.

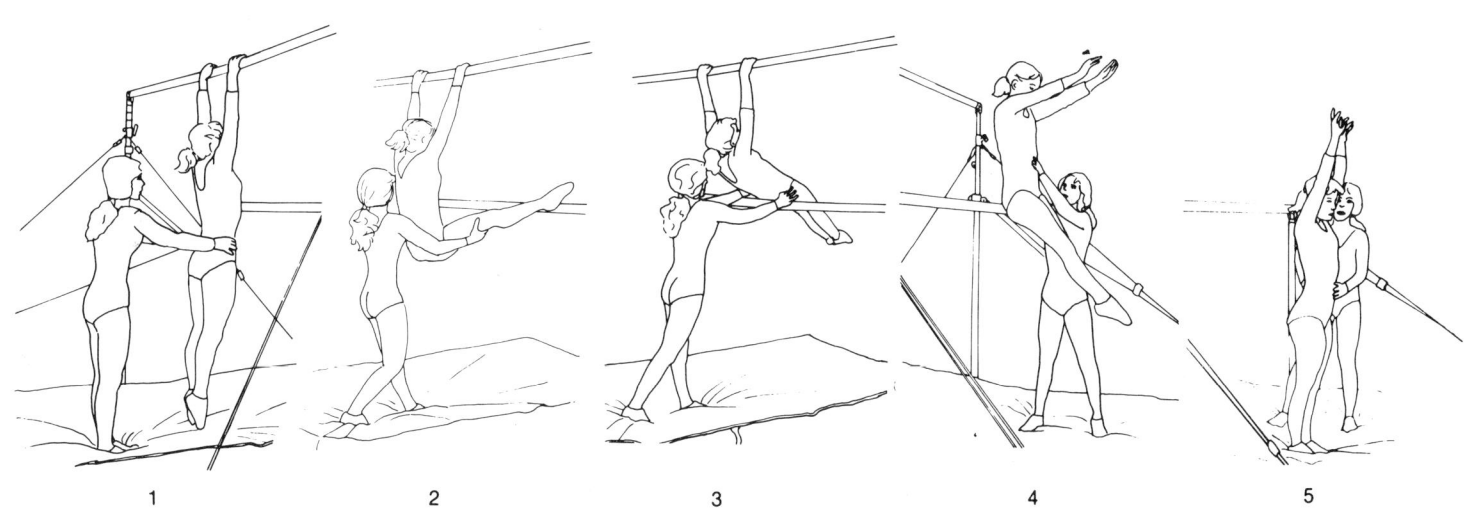

1   2   3   4   5

SKILL	DESCRIPTION	TEACHING TECHNIQUES AND OBSERVATION POINTS

Level II Skills

5. Pullover Mount to Front Support (Low Bar)

This is a good connecting skill to use in a routine to get into position for a stride circle.
1. Stand between the bars facing the low bar. Bend the elbows and grasp the low bar with a forward grip.
2. With the weight on the back foot, with one leg slightly in front of the other, step forward or shift the weight to the front foot and swing the back leg forward and upward to raise the hips to the bar.
3. As the hips move under the bar, push off with the last leg to bring the legs together over the bar.
4. Keep the elbows bent and pull the hips to the bar.
5. Lift the head and extend the arms to finish in a front support.

1. Stand close to the bar and do not allow the arms to straighten.
2. Think of swinging the leg *up* and over the bar—not outward. Hips must be kept close to the bar.
3. Once the hips are over the bar, the arms must continue to pull the hips around to the front support position.
4. Allow the hands to slide around the bar so the wrists finish over the hands for support.
5. Do not lift the head too soon. The hips must be in the front support position first.
6. Do not hesitate to lower the bar if the class is having difficulty with this skill.

Spotting
1. Stand on the opposite side of the low bar from the gymnast. Reach the near hand under the low bar and place on the gymnast's shoulder.
2. Place the other hand on her hips or upper thighs as the gymnast moves under the bar.
3. The hand on her shoulder pushes downward and then upward.
4. The hand on her hips lifts up and keeps the hips as close to the bar as possible.
5. Steady the gymnast in a front support.
6. Initially it is best to use two spotters.

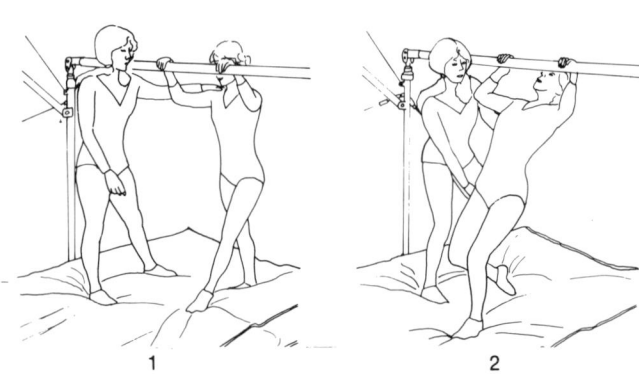

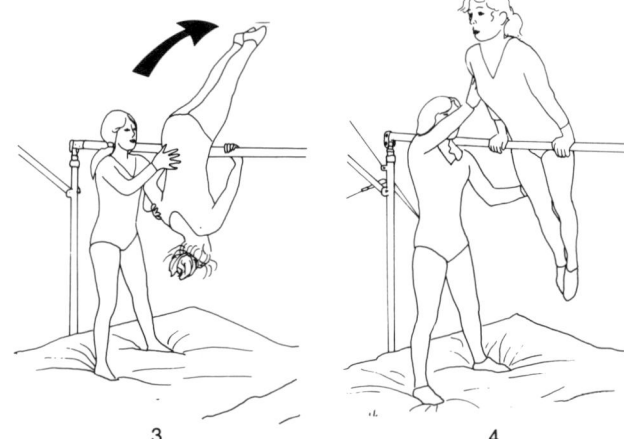

1 2 3 4

6. Front Support Swing to Stride Support

1. From a front support position (forward grip), lift the right leg upward and sideways over the low bar.

1. The gymnast will attempt to perform this without lifting her hand off the bar. Encourage her to attempt the skill properly.
2. Once this skill has been learned, it should be performed quickly.
3. Legs should be straight throughout. Hold head up.
4. The support arm must be straight, the elbow locked.

| SKILL | DESCRIPTION | TEACHING TECHNIQUES AND OBSERVATION POINTS |

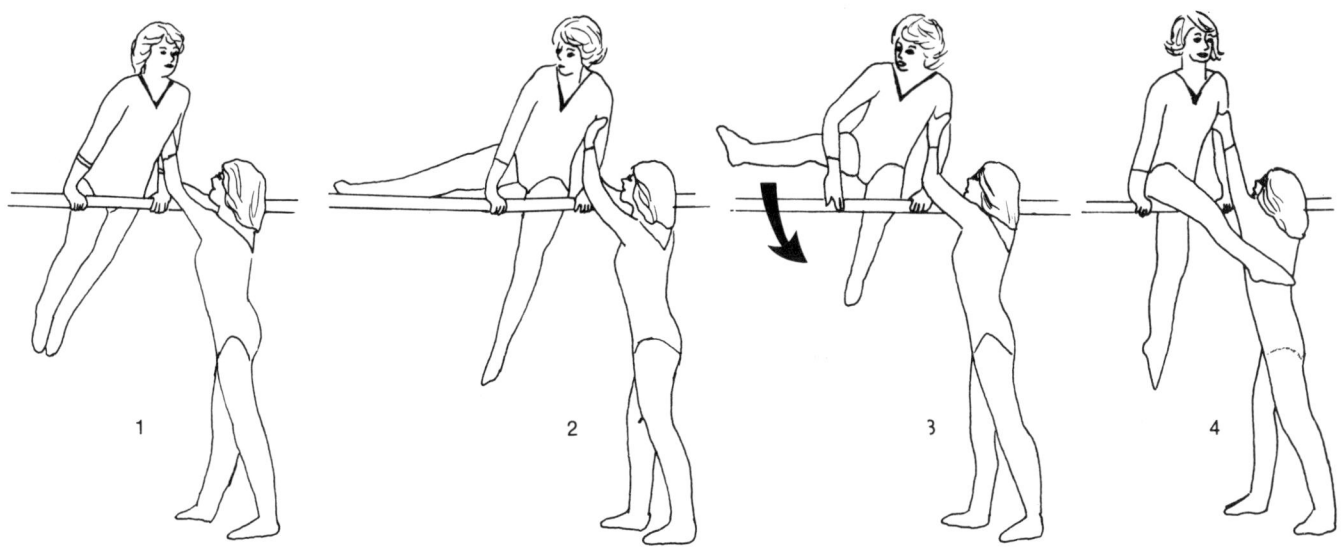

2. The right hand must be lifted off the bar to allow the legs to pass over. Immediately replace the right hand on the bar and hold the stride support. The weight is entirely on the hands.
3. Before swinging the right leg back to the original position, shift the weight to the left hand.

5. Until the stride position is reached, the shoulders should be forward of the bar.
6. Be sure the gymnasts lift the leg high enough to clear the bar.

Spotting
1. Stand on the far side of the low bar from the gymnast, and to one side.
2. Place one hand on her wrist, the other on her upper arm.
3. Steady gymnast throughout move.

7. Straddle Underswing Dismount

The girls enjoy this move. It is a little daring and exciting to do.
1. Begin in a long hang position. Straddle legs and place soles of the feet on the low bar.

1. The arms are straight throughout.
2. Tuck the head as the rotation begins.

Spotting
3. Do not take the feet off the low bar until the hips have reached the level of the low bar.

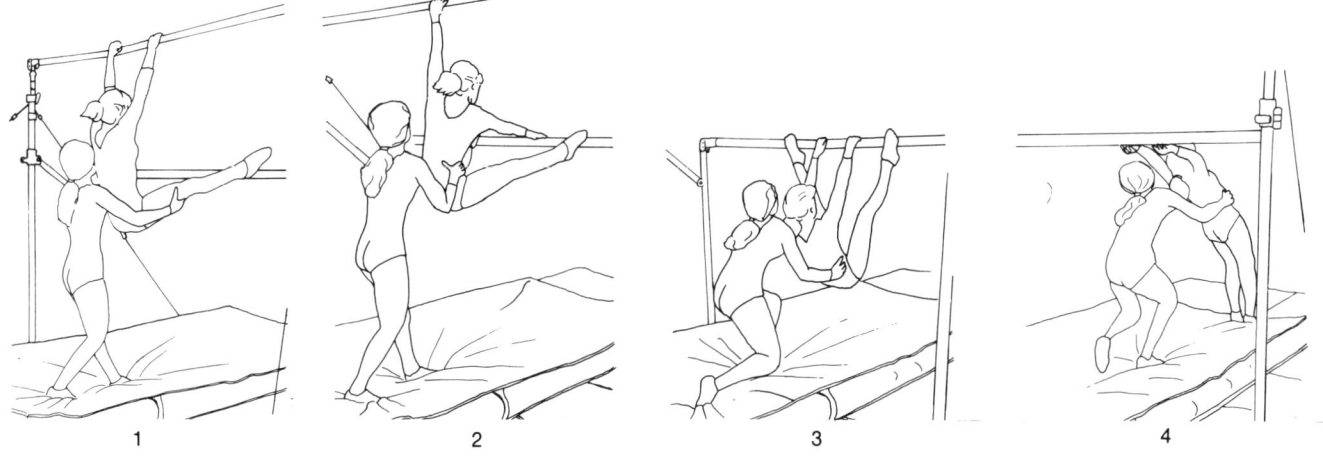

SKILL	DESCRIPTION	TEACHING TECHNIQUES AND OBSERVATION POINTS
	2. Let go of *one* hand from the high bar and place on the low bar. Release the other hand and place it on the low bar as well. This initiates the momentum and the body rotates under the low bar. 3. Once the hips have passed under the bar and continued upward in an arch, the soles of the feet come off the low bar as do the hands. The feet come together to stand on the mat.	*Spotting* 1. From the long hang position, assist the gymnast in placing her feet on the low bar. 2. Place hands on her waist and lift up to support her. If she is afraid to let go of the high bar, lift up and take her whole weight on your shoulders to let her see she is well supported. 3. When she lets go, follow her under the bar, pushing her upward as she passes under the low bar to a stand.
8. Front Support Swing (Cast)	This movement is also called a cast, and may be performed on the high or low bar. 1. From a front support position with hands in a forward grip, flex the hips, allowing the legs to come under the bar. The arms will bend slightly and the shoulders should move forward of the bar to keep the body in balance. 2. Thrust the legs backward and upward, keeping them straight and away from the bar. The arms are extended and the body returns to the bar in a slightly arched position	1. Initially the gymnasts will be reluctant to swing their legs so their hips come more than a few inches off the bar. Encourage them to swing their legs so their hips are at least thirty centimeters (1') off the bar. 2. Do not arch the body away from the bar. The body is straight during the swing, and then arches slightly before contacting the bar. 3. This is a very basic and fundamental movement for the uneven bars. Extra time spent on this skill is time well spent. *Spotting* 1. Stand to one side, behind the gymnast. Place one hand on her wrist and the other under her thigh. 2. Assist the gymnast by lifting her body away from the bar.

1

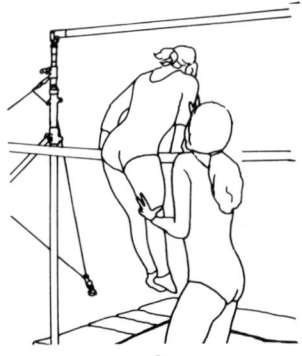
2

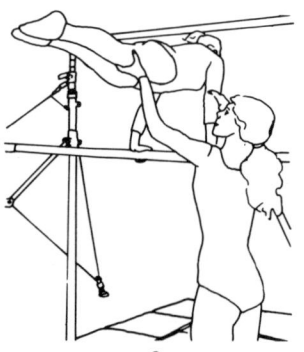
3

SKILL	DESCRIPTION	TEACHING TECHNIQUES AND OBSERVATION POINTS
9. Back Hip Circle	1. Perform a cast as described above. 2. As soon as the body contacts the bar, flex the hips, allowing the legs to come under the bar. The arms will flex slightly to keep the hips close to the bar. 3. Rotate around the bar and then extend the arms to finish in the original position.	1. After the cast, contact the bar with the lower abdominal area where the hip naturally flexes. 2. The cast must be high enough to give the legs momentum to get the body around the bar. 3. The body should pike *as* the hips meet the bar. Do not pike too soon, however. 4. The hands must rotate around the bar. 5. Legs are straight throughout. *Spotting* 1. Stand on the opposite side of the bar from the gymnast. 2. Reach one hand under the bar and place on her hips. 3. As the gymnast finishes the cast and her hips contact the bar, assist the gymnast in keeping her hips to the bar. 4. As her legs rotate under the bar, place the other hand on her upper thigh and lift her legs up and over the bar. 5. Steady the gymnast in the support position.

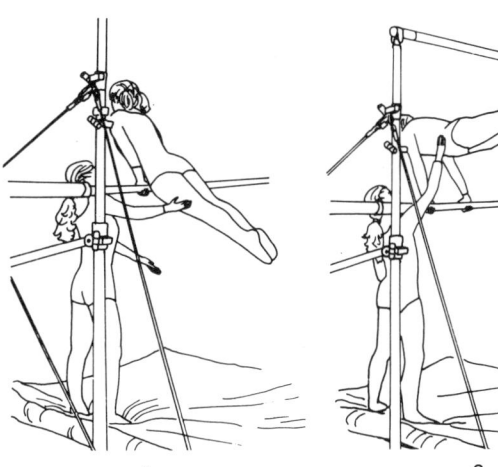
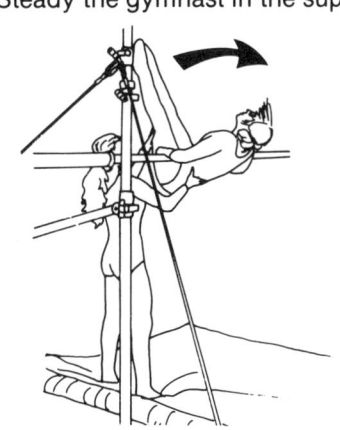
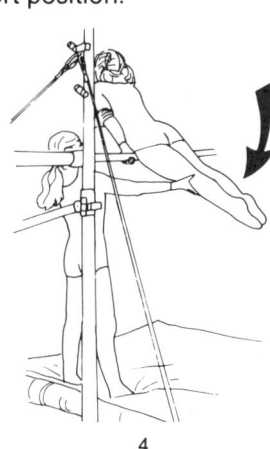

1   2   3   4

Level III Skills

10. Single Knee Drop and Back to Stride Support	1. From a stride support position on the low bar, hands in a forward grip, lift the weight off the bar with straight arms.	1. Keep arms straight and the body away from the bar during the downswing. 2. Keeping the legs straight is the secret to getting back up. Use a pumping action. 3. Allow the hands to rotate around the bar and then back up to the position used for the original stride support.

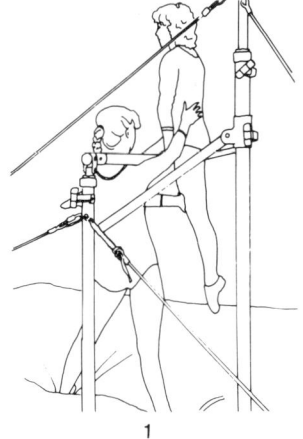
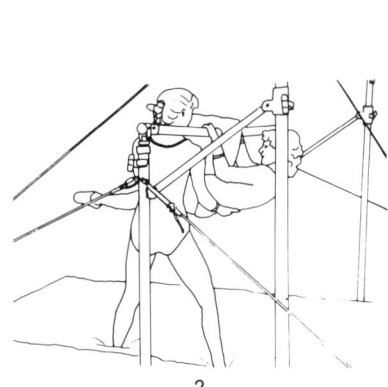
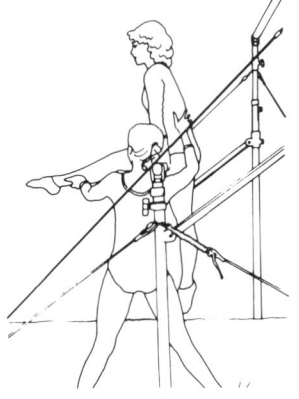

1   2   3

SKILL	DESCRIPTION	TEACHING TECHNIQUES AND OBSERVATION POINTS
	2. Swing the rear leg backward and upward, at the same time bending the front knee so it hooks around the bar. 3. Swing back and under the low bar, being careful to control the momentum. 4. Swing the rear leg down, forcing the body to come back to the stride position.	*Spotting* 1. Stand between the bars, with one hand on the gymnast's upper back, the other reaching under the bar to be placed on the upper thigh of her rear leg. 2. Support the gymnast as she falls back, and assist with the pumping action on her rear leg as she returns to the stride support. 3. Steady her in the stride position.
11. Stride Circle Forward	1. Begin in a stride support, hands in a reverse grip. 2. Lift the body off the bar so the weight is on the hands. Hold the head and chest up. 3. Initiate the movement of the body around the bar by reaching out with the lead foot as if you are going to take a step forward. The hips come forward as well so that the bar is touching the rear leg. Keep the legs as far apart as possible throughout the movement. 4. Finish in a stride support.	*Spotting* 1. Stand behind the gymnast, to one side. Reach under the low bar to place your hand on the gymnast's back, palm facing away. If you are unable to reach her back, grasp her wrist. 2. Assist the gymnast in initiating momentum by applying pressure as she moves around the bar. As the gymnast reaches the original position, stop her forward leg in a stride position, thus keeping her from continuing on around the bar.

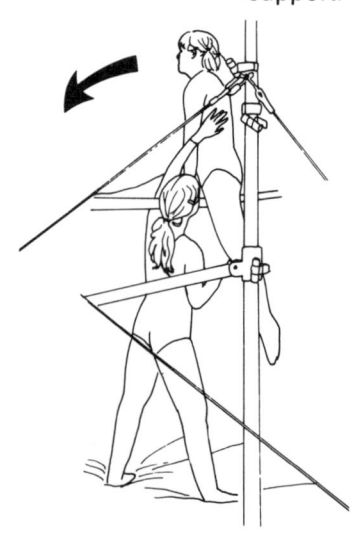

1

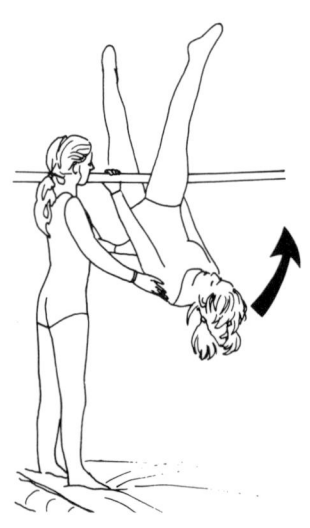

2

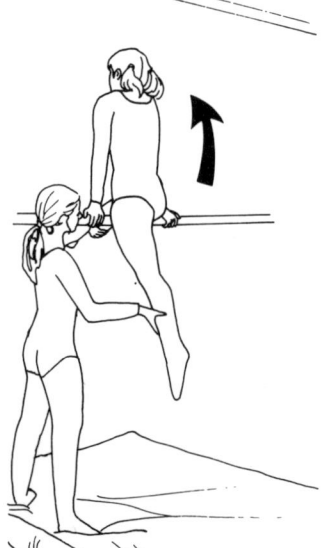

| SKILL | DESCRIPTION | TEACHING TECHNIQUES AND OBSERVATION POINTS |

12. Stride Circle Re-grasp (High Bar)

This skill is performed in the same manner as the stride circle
1. When the body is inverted, the gymnast should begin to look for the high bar.
2. Just before the original position is reached, grasp the high bar with both hands simultaneously, keeping the body straight.

1. This is one of the first re-grasp moves to be introduced.
2. The gymnast must be able to perform a good stride circle alone so the spotter need only be concerned with the re-grasp part of the skill.
3. Be careful not to reach for the high bar too soon. It is better to be slightly late than early.
4. Have the gymnast perform a stride circle giving a verbal cue when the re-grasp should take place. This will assist the gymnast with proper timing.
5. Keep the hips moving forward throughout the skill. Think of the skill as a full stride circle, not a three-quarter one.

Spotting
1. Spotting is the same as for the stride circle with hand placement on the gymnast's back. Follow the gymnast as she moves around the bar and then, using both hands, give additional support to her back while she reaches for the high bar.
2. Sometimes, while the gymnast is moving her hands from the low bar to the high bar, she swings them sideways hitting the spotter in the face. To reduce the incidence of this, have the gymnast grasp the high bar in the correct stride position. While the spotter stands behind with both her hands supporting the gymnast's back, the gymnast practices moving her hands alternately from the low bar to the high bar.
   Note: The gymnast must be able to maintain the straight back position.
3. Two spotters should be used initially.

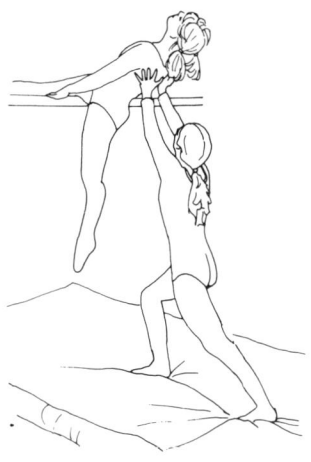

1

2

SKILL	DESCRIPTION	TEACHING TECHNIQUES AND OBSERVATION POINTS

13. Pullover to High Bar

This is one of the most common methods of moving from the low bar to the high bar.
1. Grasp the high bar with the regular grip.
2. Bend the knee and place one foot on the low bar, while the other leg remains straight and extended over the low bar.
3. Swing the straight leg up over the high bar while at the same time bending the arms to get hips to the high bar.
4. Push with the bent leg to bring legs together and finish in a front support position on the high bar.

1. The gymnast should be able to perform a pullover mount on the low bar before attempting one on the high bar.
2. The hands must rotate around the high bar as the body moves to the front support position.
3. The skill is more easily performed if the distance between the bars is reduced. The distance can be increased once the gymnast has mastered the skill.

Spotting
1. Initially it may be preferable to spot this skill from an elevated position, such as the top of the Swedish box.
2. Stand between the bars to one side of the gymnast.
3. Assist by pushing the gymnast's hips to the high bar.
4. Grasp the ankles to help the gymnast steady herself in the front support position.

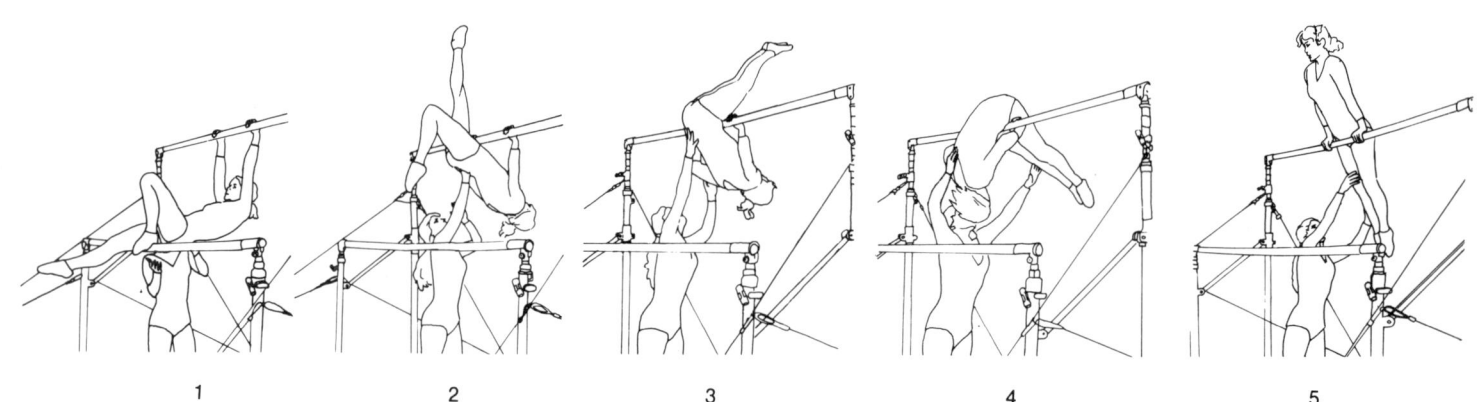

1 2 3 4 5

SKILL	DESCRIPTION	TEACHING TECHNIQUES AND OBSERVATION POINTS
14. Pike Drop from High Bar to Low Bar	1. From a front support position on the high bar, with hands in a regular grip and the hips kept close to the high bar, allow the upper body to drop back. 2. As the body moves under the bar the arms bend slightly. The legs should be together and in a piked position. 3. Once the hips are over the low bar, lower the legs so that the hips rest on the low bar. Hands continue to grip the high bar.	1. This is a good basic method for moving from the high bar to the low bar. 2. This skill should be practiced on the low bar so the gymnast may experience the feeling of dropping the upper body backward without the added fear of height. 3. If performed correctly, there is a smooth, even rhythm to this skill. 4. This may also be used as a dismount off the high bar (in the direction away from the low bar), or off the low bar. 5. Arms must be straight as the body drops backward. 6. The legs must be lowered from the pike position to the low bar with control. *Spotting* 1. Stand between the bars to one side of the gymnast. 2. Support her hips with one hand and her thighs with the other, being careful not to get a hand caught between the bar and her thighs as they come to rest on the low bar. 3. Assist the gymnast by controlling the speed of her legs.

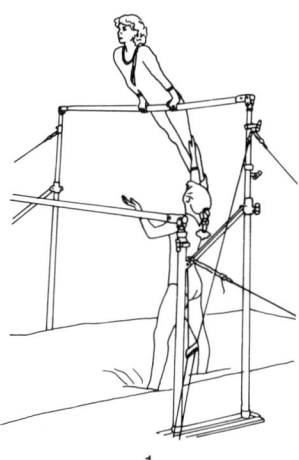 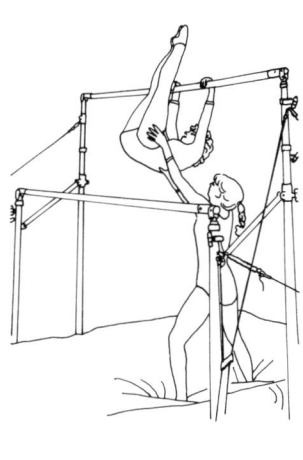 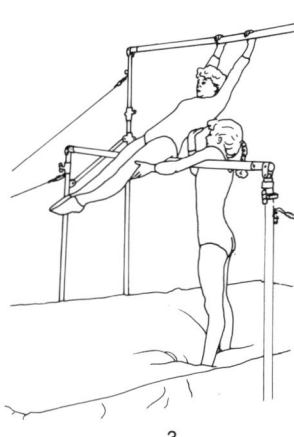

1 2 3

15. Double Leg Stem Rise to High Bar	1. Grasp the high bar with both hands in the regular grip. Place the balls of the feet on the low bar, legs bent. 2. Forcefully extend the legs, raising the hips to the high bar. The elbows bend slightly to let the shoulders pass over the high bar.	1. Use the strength of the arms to pull downward forcefully on the high bar, forcing the hips upward. 2. Move the bars closer than usual until the correct action has been learned. 3. Keep the feet on the low bar until the body has almost reached the front support position. 4. To coordinate the thrust of the legs and the pull of the arms correctly, the gymnast should think of moving out, around, and then on top of the high bar.

SKILL	DESCRIPTION	TEACHING TECHNIQUES AND OBSERVATION POINTS

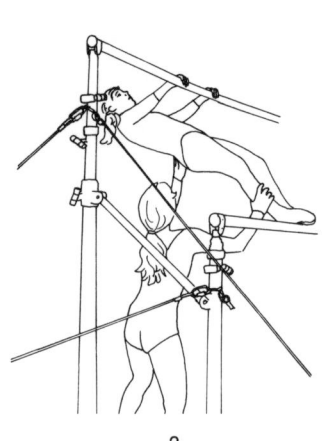 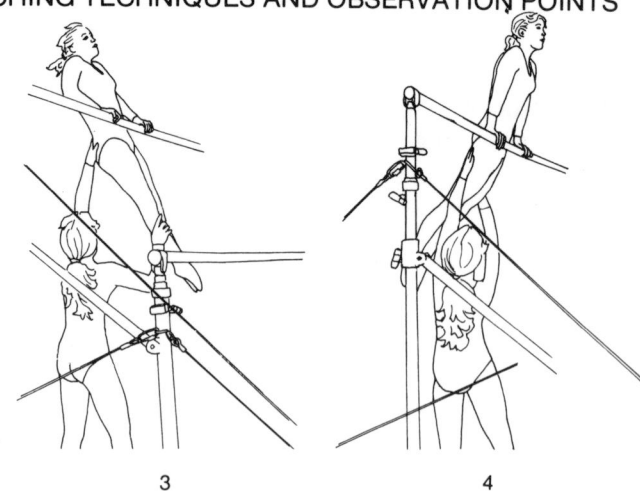

1   2   3   4

	3. Allow the hands to move around and on top of the high bar, finishing in a front support.	*Spotting* 1. Stand under the high bar to one side of the gymnast. 2. Place one hand on her hip, the other on her ankle. 3. Assist the gymnast in moving backward and then upward to the high bar. 4. Spotting from an elevated position will enable the spotter to give better assistance.
16. Cast from High Bar to Feint Wrap on Low Bar a) To Determine Bar Width:	1. Begin in a long hang position on the high bar. The spotter stands between the bars and initiates the swing. 2. As the gymnast comes in contact with the low bar, she forcefully pikes around the low bar, bringing her toes as close to her nose as possible. 3. The spotter should assist by placing one hand on the gymnast's back to force her hips to the low bar, and the other hand under her upper thigh to assist with raising the legs to the pike position.	1. The movement in this skill should be smooth and painless. To ensure this, it will be necessary to determine the bar width for each individual, that is, the distance the bars must be apart so the gymnast can grasp the high bar and swing to a piked position around the low bar. 2. This should be a comfortable exercise for the gymnast so the distance between the bars should be increased or decreased to accommodate each girl. 3. Encourage students to remember the numerical position for their bar width to help save time in making bar adjustments. 4. A towel or piece of foam rubber secured with masking tape is useful for cushioning in the early stages of this skill.

SKILL	DESCRIPTION	TEACHING TECHNIQUES AND OBSERVATION POINTS
b) Cast to Long Hang	This is the next stage in learning the Cast to Feint Wrap. 1. Begin in a front support position on the high bar. Bring the legs under the high bar as described earlier in the Front Support Swing. 2. Force the legs backward and upward, at the same time extending the arms to push the body away from the high bar. 3. Tuck the head between straight arms and keep the body in a fully extended position, legs together and straight. This body position is very often referred to as "tight." 4. All body muscles should be controlled and pulled in.	1. This skill should be attempted on the low bar first. Two spotters, one on either side, should stop the gymnast in midair when she is fully extended. Corrections can easily be seen from this position. 2. Arms must be fully extended to avoid the jarring effect that occurs when the entire body weight is supported by bent arms. *Spotting* 1. Two spotters are preferable with this skill. 2. Stand under the high bar and focus on the lower body of the gymnast. As she extends her body and swings down toward the low bar, grasp her with one arm around her abdomen, supporting her with your body and shoulder. 3. The second spotter should assist as a back up to the first, should she miss her grip.
c). Cast from High Bar to Feint Wrap on Low Bar	After learning these two lead-up skills, the entire move can be performed.	1. Both lead-ups should be learned prior to attempting the complete skill. 2. As you approach the low bar from the long hang, lead with the hips in a slightly arched position. 3. Be sure the high bar is not slippery and the hands have sufficient chalk on them.

 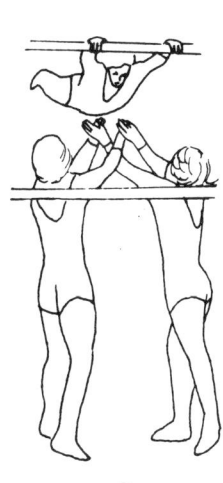 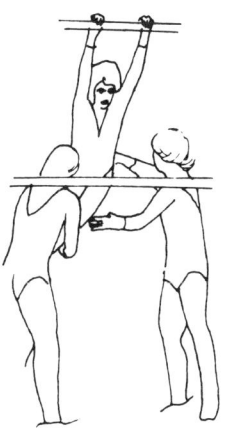 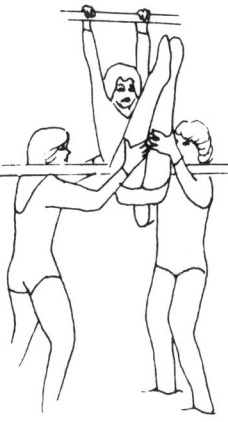

1   2   3   4

SKILL	DESCRIPTION	TEACHING TECHNIQUES AND OBSERVATION POINTS
		Spotting 1. Implement the spotting techniques as described earlier for the different aspects of the skill. 2. Stand between the bars and to one side of the gymnast. 3. As the gymnast approaches the low bar, slow down her swing if necessary, so she contacts the bar in the correct position at a reasonable speed. 4. Assist her with the full pike position around the low bar. 5. Discuss with the gymnast the contact with the bar and make the necessary adjustments. Keep in mind that as the gymnast relaxes and fully extends her body, the distance will need to be *increased*. Remember, it is better for the bar to be too close than too far apart for safety reasons.
17. Thigh Pivot Turn	1. This skill is also known as Skin the Cat to Rear Support. 2. Begin by sitting on the low bar, hands gripping the high bar in a regular grip. 3. Taking the weight on the hands, raise the feet to the high bar, putting the feet through the hands to an inverted position (legs straight). This part of the skill is known as a "skin the cat." 4. Allow the hips to come through the arms as the legs slide slowly along the low bar to mid-thigh.	1. Have the gymnast perform this on the low bar first, to determine which hand she will release and to allow her to experience the inverted position and the rotation. 2. Demand that the gymnast move through this skill slowly and with control. 3. Do not slide past the mid-thigh or she will rotate and the bar will be on the small of her back, instead of her upper thighs. 4. Before releasing the hands, lower the hips so the body is slightly arched. *Spotting* 1. Initially, stand between the bars to one side of the gymnast and assist her in raising her legs to the inverted position. Lower her legs slowly to the low bar to the middle of her thighs. 2. Move under the high bar, facing the low bar, and support the gymnast's shoulder to give her confidence before she releases one hand.

1   2   3   4   5

SKILL	DESCRIPTION	TEACHING TECHNIQUES AND OBSERVATION POINTS
	5. Release one hand and allow the body to rotate around to a sitting position on the low bar. Grasp the high bar with the free hand and change the grip of the other hand to a regular grip.	3. Assist the gymnast to rotate by placing the hands on her waist.
18. Routine	1. Front support mount (facing the high bar) 2. Swing leg to stride support 3. Single knee drop 4. Swing rear leg to sit on low bar facing high bar 5. Thigh pivot turn 6. Pullover from low bar to high bar 7. Pike drop from high bar to low bar 8. Straddle underswing dismount	1. The performing of several uneven bar skills together can be very tiring. Gymnasts should take care not to attempt too many skills together at once. 2. After each skill has been learned individually, and can be performed to the best of the gymnast's ability, begin with the first three movements of the routine, adding one new element after the combined skills are performed easily. The routine should be performed without pauses and correct form stressed.

Level IV Skills

19. Front Hip Circle	1. Begin in a front support position. Hands in a regular grip. 2. Extend body so the bar is high on the upper thighs. Hold head and chest high, lean outward keeping upper body extended. 3. Just as the body reaches the inverted position, or a loss of balance is experienced, forcefully pike the upper body around the bar.	1. Total body extension is needed for this skill. 2. Hands must rotate around the bar. 3. Legs are straight throughout. 4. Timing is important. Piking too late or too soon will break the momentum of the skill. 5. The body remains in contact with the bar throughout the skill. 6. Gymnasts should practice performing a high swing after this skill. This prepares them for additional combinations using this skill.

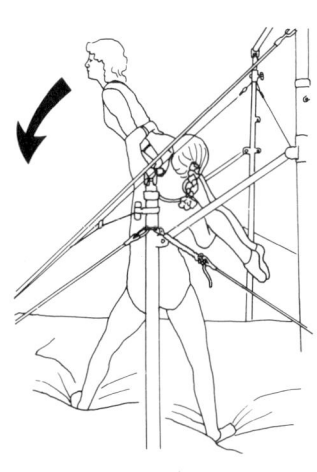

1

2

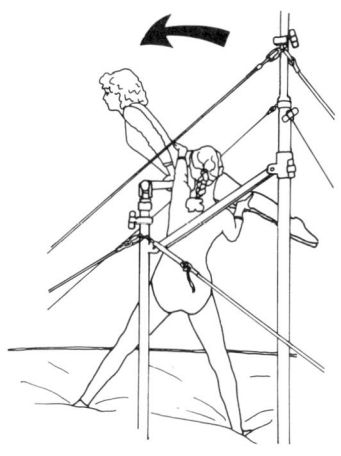

3

SKILL	DESCRIPTION	TEACHING TECHNIQUES AND OBSERVATION POINTS
	4. Bend elbows slightly so that the body rotates around the bar and back to the original position.	*Spotting* 1. Use two spotters, both standing between the bars, one on either side of the gymnast. 2. Reach under the bar and place one hand on the lower back and hips. 3. Assist the gymnast with the correct timing by applying pressure at the moment at which piking should occur. 4. As the gymnast rotates under the bar, place the other hand on her back and assist her with a high swing. Steady in a front support.
20. **Single Leg Stem Rise**	1. Begin as for the double leg stem rise. 2. Extend one leg so the ankle contacts the high bar. The other leg should be bent and on the low bar. 3. Extend the bent leg and drive the hips backward and upward. 4. Keeping the arms straight, force down with the hands on the high bar bringing the hips to the high bar. Rotate the grip and finish in a front support position.	1. See teaching technique discussion for the double leg stem rise. 2. Have the gymnast imagine she is pulling on a pair of jeans, by pulling the bar all along the raised straight leg. 3. The foot of the bent leg *remains* on the low bar until the front support position is ready to be assumed. *Spotting* As for the double leg stem rise.

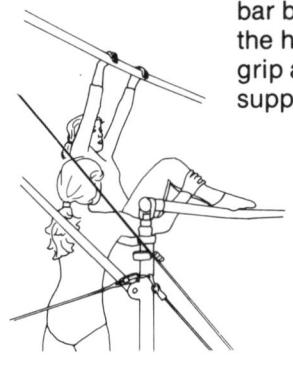
1

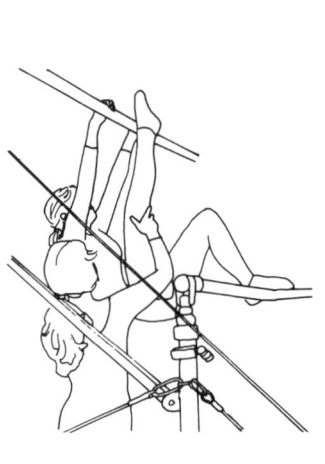
2

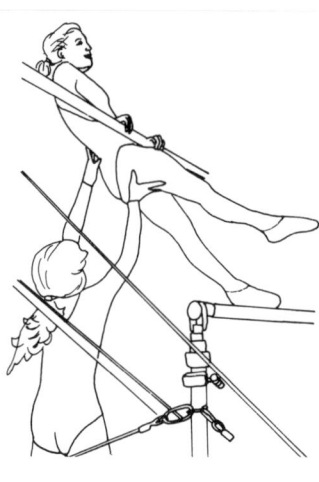
3

| 21. **Cast From High Bar to Wrap Around Low Bar** | 1. This skill is performed exactly as described for the cast from the high bar to feint wrap.
2. At the point where the gymnast is in a full pike around the low bar, the performer releases the high bar to *re-grasp* the low bar and continues with a hip circle around the low bar. | 1. This is an advanced skill and is rarely taught in the classroom. It is included here for teachers who have very talented gymnasts to work with. Proper progressions must be used to prepare the gymnast for this skill. Please refer to the progressions described for the cast from high bar to feint wrap on low bar (see page 56).
2. The gymnast should be able to perform a back hip circle and the cast from the high bar to feint wrap around the low bar.
3. It is important to remember that the gymnast does not release the high bar until she can wrap herself around the low bar in a tight pike position. |

SKILL	DESCRIPTION	TEACHING TECHNIQUES AND OBSERVATION POINTS

3. Finish in a front support position.

4. In the initial stages the gymnast may anticipate the wrap and begin to pike too soon. She should lead with hips out of the cast. After the hips make contact, thrust the legs upward into the pike position.
5. This skill should not be attempted without a landing pad.
6. Briefly, the progressions should be as follows:
   a) Gymnast should already be able to perform the support swing and back hip circle.
   b) Support swing from low bar into arms of spotter. Catch at horizontal.
   c) Cast from high bar. Spotters must stop gymnast from hitting low bar.
   d) From long hang practice feint wraps (swinging into low bar and piking around bar) with spotter.
   e) After two feint wraps, wrap the third time and release high bar to hip circle around low bar.
   f) From high bar cast to long hang to feint wrap around low bar. Spotter can slow cast down to make wrap painless until gymnast can do it on her own.
   g) Cast from high bar to hip circle around low bar.

Spotting
1. See description of spotting for cast from high bar to feint wrap on low bar (see page 57).
2. Stand to one side, between the bars. As the gymnast approaches, place one hand on her back to bring the hips to the bar, the other hand under her thighs to wrap her legs in a pike position. Steady in a front support.
3. A second spotter can assist by standing in front of the low bar and helping the gymnast with the hip circle part of the skill. A third spotter can also duplicate the spotting in the first description.
4. Verbal cues are sometimes helpful in the early stages.
5. Spotter should be careful of the gymnast's hands as they re-grasp the low bar. Sometimes they move sideways on their way to the bar.

22. Optional Routine

Design a routine using skills appropriate to the gymnast's ability. Length is optional.

1. When designing an uneven parallel bar routine, one must consider the following:
   a) Utilize both the high and low bars.
   b) Do not pause between skills.
   c) A re-grasp movement (a movement which requires the gymnast to let go with both hands simultaneously and then re-grasp the same bar or the other bar) should be included.
   d) The routine should begin with a mount and end with a dismount.
   e) Do not repeat skills.
2. Some students may have difficulty getting their routines started. Allow them to use the Level III routine and change various skills to ones more appropriate to their ability and preference.
3. Have the students practice their judging on each other's routines.

| SKILL | DESCRIPTION | TEACHING TECHNIQUES AND OBSERVATION POINTS |

C. Balance Beam

The creative capacity of the balance beam is unlimited and many girls find this to be the most attractive aspect of this event. This 10 cm (4") wide, 5 meter (16') long piece of wood presents a challenge to the student because it requires courage, and body control over a small base of support. Many of the skills learned in tumbling and dance have direct application to the balance beam.

General Safety

1. It is important to check the apparatus before each lesson to see that all supports are securely fastened.
2. If the equipment has to be transported from a storage area, care must be taken in moving it from one place to another. Feet must be kept clear when moving the balance beam, and if the supports are lowered to the floor, this must be done with care.
3. The locking devices for controlling the height of the beam should be checked and care taken in lowering and raising the apparatus.
4. Mats should be placed under and around the beam. A double thickness of mats should be provided for dismounts.
5. If a beat board is to be used for mounts, its position on the floor should be secure. It should be removed immediately after the gymnast has mounted the apparatus.
6. Footwear is a very important consideration for safety reasons. Any slippery footwear must be removed. It is best to perform on this apparatus with bare feet or gymnastics slippers.
7. If two people are working on the beam at one time, care must be taken that each is aware of the other.
8. Gymnasts should progress from a line on the floor, to a bench, to a low beam, and finally the beam should be raised to the suggested practice height of one meter (3').
9. When a gymnast is learning new skills, a spotter should stand on each side of the beam. As the gymnast gains more confidence in performing the skill, only one spotter may be needed.

Note: Since many of the skills have been previously discussed in the Floor Exercise section, only information relevant to the beam will be included.

Level I Skills

1. Forward Walking

1. From a standing position on the beam, extend the right leg, turning the foot out, then place the toes on the beam and lower the heel.
2. Repeat with the left leg, moving down the length of the beam.

1. Hold head up and focus the eyes on the end of the beam.
2. Participants who feel very nervous on the beam should run their feet along so they can feel where they must place their foot.
3. By keeping the shoulders down and the abdomen tucked in, wobbling is kept to a minimum.
4. In the early stages, participants may find it more relaxing to keep their arms out at the sides.
5. Take small steps.
6. Have the students vary the walk. High and low variations. Fast and slow.

SKILL	DESCRIPTION	TEACHING TECHNIQUES AND OBSERVATION POINTS
	3. Arms are held in a "V" above the head. Body must be firm, in correct body alignment.	*Spotting* 1. Spotters walk, one on either side, beside the gymnast, with their arms extended toward the gymnast. 2. If the gymnast should need spotting, it is best that *she reach* for the spotters for support.
2. Backward Walking	1. From a standing position on the beam, extend the right foot backward, placing the toe on the beam and then the entire foot. 2. Repeat for the left leg. 3. Arms as for the forward walk.	1. To assist the participant with correct foot placement, have each girl run her toes along the side of the beam as she extends the foot backward. This helps her to "feel" the beam. 2. Correct body alignment is essential. 3. Eyes focus on the end of the beam. 4. Take small even steps. 5. Vary the walk as for the forward walk.
3. Front Support Mount to Stand	1. Stand facing the beam. Place hands on beam with fingertips facing away from body. 2. Jump to front support position with arms straight, body straight, thighs resting against the beam. 3. Lift the right leg sideways up and over the beam to a straddle sit position. 4. Swing legs backward to place toes on the beam to a squat position. Raise arms to a horizontal position and come to a stand, arms above head.	1. The beam will have to be high enough so participants can support themselves. 2. Hands are placed close together so leg can be swung around in a controlled manner. 3. Do not allow participants to rise to a stand until the hands have been raised to a horizontal position. 4. This is a very basic mount. 5. Legs are straight throughout until the squat position is reached. 6. Arms are straight during backswing of legs to squat position. 7. Two gymnasts can work on this mount at once, one at either end. *Spotting* 1. Stand on the opposite side of the beam from the gymnast. Support her upper body by placing hands around her upper arms. 2. Keep head well back and out of reach of the gymnast as she jumps forward. 3. Continue to support and guide gymnast through the straddle sit to the standing position.

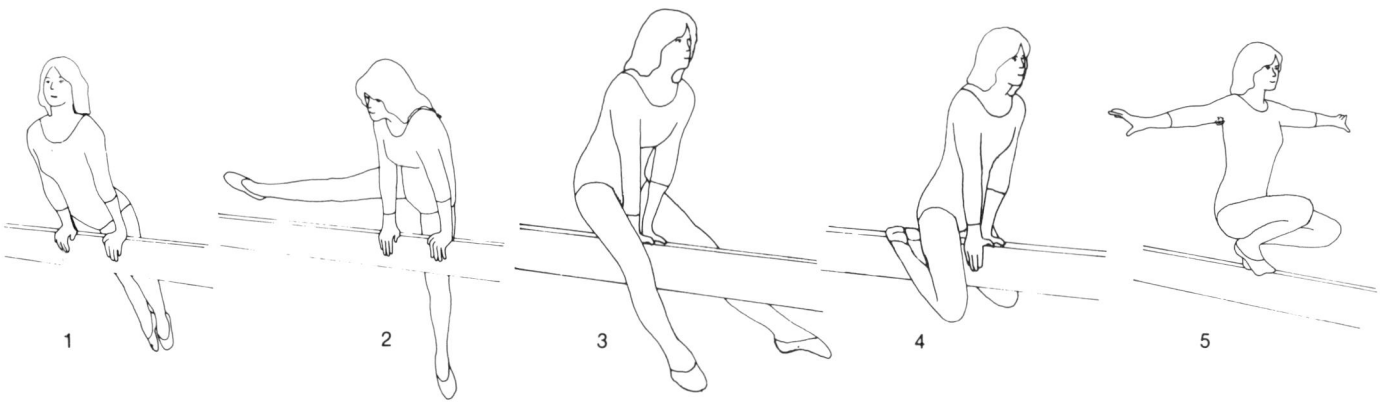

1   2   3   4   5

SKILL	DESCRIPTION	TEACHING TECHNIQUES AND OBSERVATION POINTS
4. Knee Scale 	1. This is a static position or a pose and need only be held long enough to show that there is control and balance has been attained. 2. A good guide is to have the gymnasts count slowly to three. 3. The particular body position can be determined from the accompanying illustration.	1. The raised leg should be straight and raised as high as possible. 2. Elbows should be locked, thumbs together and fingers along the outside of the beam. 3. Keep the head up. 4. The instep of the bent leg is down along the top of the beam. 5. To get out of this position, lower the raised leg and straddle the beam in a straddle sit position. *Spotting* 1. Initially, two spotters should be used, one on either side of the beam. 2. Support the upper arm and keep the hips over the beam.
5. Two-Foot Jumps 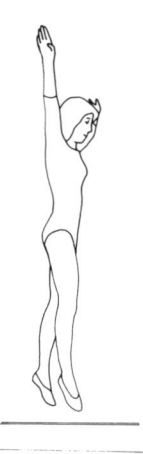	1. Begin with one foot ahead of the other, toes turned outward. 2. Bend the knees slightly, and then extend the legs forcefully to lift the body off the beam, legs straight and together, feet extended toward the beam. 3. Land toes first, flexing the knees again upon touching the beam. Upper body is held erect and arms are lowered for the take off and then are raised overhead to give the impression of height.	1. As always, begin on the floor and do not use slippery footwear. 2. Participants should begin with low jumps and as they gain more confidence, attempt higher jumps. 3. Keep eyes focused on the beam. 4. Legs are kept as close together as possible while the body is lifted above the beam. *Spotting* 1. Stand on either side of the beam and extend hand to gymnast.
6. One-Half Turn on Toes of Two Feet 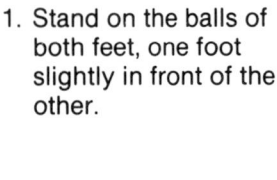  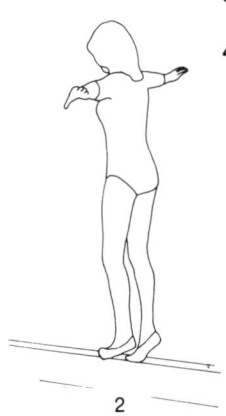 1 2	1. Stand on the balls of both feet, one foot slightly in front of the other.	1. Feet must not be too far apart. To ensure that they are close together, begin by stepping forward on the *toes* of one foot and then bring the other foot, on the toes, in behind. 2. Spot the other end of the beam after the turn. 3. Keep the knees and thighs pressed together to help keep the body erect. 4. Remember to turn *toward* the rear foot.

SKILL	DESCRIPTION	TEACHING TECHNIQUES AND OBSERVATION POINTS

| | 2. Holding the head up, initiate the turn with the hips and upper body. Rotate 180° to face the opposite direction, turning toward the back foot. | 5. Arm position is optional, but suggested position is above the head or held out from the sides.

Spotting
1. The spotter stands beside the beam, arm extended. |
| **7. Forward Roll with Spotting** | 1. Begin in a squat position, one foot ahead of the other. Place hands on top of the beam approximately 30 cm (12") ahead of the feet, tucking the head close to the body so the roll takes place on the upper back.
2. As the weight is taken on the shoulders, immediately slide the hands to the underside of the beam, pressing both elbows against the head.
3. Maintaining the pike position as long as possible, lower the hips to the beam, keeping the legs vertical until the hips are securely placed on the beam.
4. Sit up, at the same time lowering the legs to a straddle sit position. | 1. The nature of balance beam routines is such that tumbling elements must be incorporated into the routine in such a way that the continuity is not broken. There must be no major breaks. A forward roll done in this manner is an advanced skill and can be called a continuous forward roll. (See Level IV). The slowing down of this forward roll is for safety purposes and this also makes it suitable for the Level I gymnast.
2. Control is the major concern. This skill should be practiced on the mats first. Initially participants will want to lift the head immediately, before the hips are securely placed. Insist that students demonstrate control before coming to a sitting position. See illustration below.
3. Draw chalk lines on the mats and have participants perform forward rolls over the chalk to see if the chalk line runs down the center of their backs.
4. Keep a close eye on the progressions and techniques of each gymnast. Check each progression on the floor and bench before allowing gymnasts to progress to the beam.
5. Hips must be high enough to enable the performer to tuck the head between the arms.
6. Roll slowly, with control.
7. Maintain the pike as long as possible, legs straight.
8. Sit up as the legs come down. |

  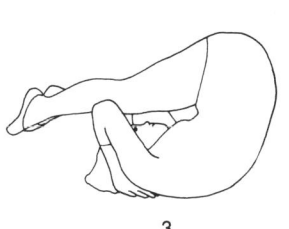 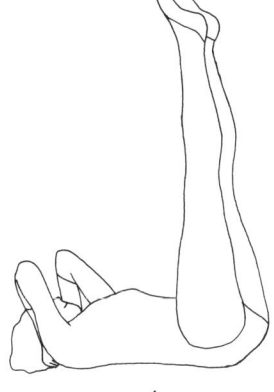

1   2   3   4

SKILL	DESCRIPTION	TEACHING TECHNIQUES AND OBSERVATION POINTS

Spotting
1. Use two spotters, one on either side of the beam.
2. Spotter faces the gymnast, with one hip against the beam.
3. Reach over the gymnast's head to place both hands on the gymnast's hips. Sometimes just as the gymnast tucks her head, she forgets to push forward with her legs to direct the roll. The spotter must have a good hold on the hips of the gymnast and assist the gymnast in following through by pulling the hips toward the spotter.
4. As the gymnast rolls, the spotters guide the hips onto the beam, watching that the legs remain straight and in the piked position.
5. Steady the gymnast and assist her in coming to a sitting position by lifting her shoulders.
6. Spotters should check to see that the elbows are tight to the head, the hips are securely placed on the beam, and hands are under the beam, before assisting the performer to a straddle sit position.

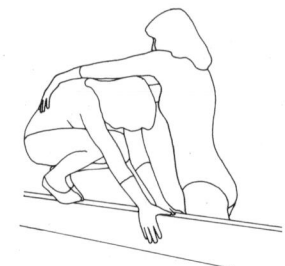
1

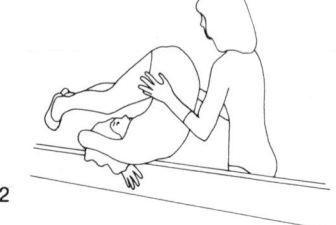
2

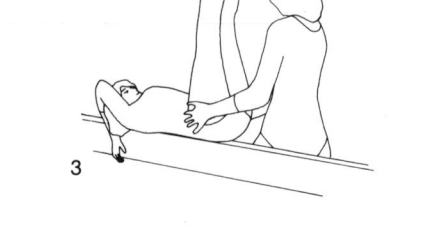
3

8. Straight Jump Dismount

1. With the feet together, flex the knees and then forcefully extend them, jumping upward and forward away from the beam. The body is fully extended while in the air.
2. Use the arms to gain maximum elevation by lowering them as the knees bend and raising them as the extension takes place.

1. This may be performed off the end of the beam or sideways. Be sure to have additional mats placed for the dismount.
2. In all dismounts, the landing should be with a flexed knee to absorb the shock and to help maintain a balanced position. Performers should be encouraged to hold a balanced position for a count of three before stepping away from the apparatus.
3. Be sure the legs are extended when the jump takes place.
4. Push from the balls of the feet.
5. Jump up *and* away from the beam.

Spotting
1. Two spotters may be necessary, one to keep the gymnast away from the beam and another to keep the gymnast from falling forward on the landing.

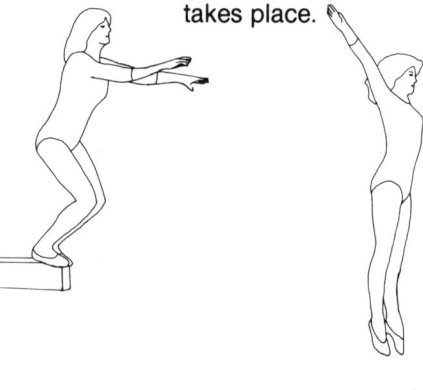

1 　 2 　 3 　 4

SKILL	DESCRIPTION	TEACHING TECHNIQUES AND OBSERVATION POINTS

Level II Skills

9. Chassé

Please see the description in the Floor Exercise section on page 29.

1. As in all skills on the balance beam, the skill should be perfected on the floor before moving to the beam.
2. Initially, the use of the arms should be optional. As the gymnast becomes more confident, the instructor may wish to suggest a specific placement of the arms, such as in a "V" above the head.
3. Height and distance are important in this movement.

Spotting
1. The spotter should stand beside the beam with arms outstretched.

10. Running Forward

1. Running on the beam should be worked up to gradually, beginning with an elongated walking step.
2. From there move to a faster elongated walking step incorporating a slight leap between steps.

1. Running on the beam involves varying degrees of difficulty depending on the speed. Gymnasts must work within their abilities.
2. Stress practice on the floor, benches and low beam before progressing to the regulation beam.
3. Participants must be familiar with the beam before attempting to run on it. They should be aware of its length and width, and how smooth its surface is.
4. Beware of slippery footwear.

11. Straddle Mount

1. Place hands on beam and jump to straight arm support, at the same time extending the legs sideways in a straddle position.
2. The shoulders move slightly forward of the hand position. Keep the head up.

1. The hips must be raised high enough to allow the feet to be placed on the beam.
2. Begin with the beam low enough to enable the gymnast to perform this mount easily. Then gradually raise the beam.
3. Some gymnasts may need to use the beat board to get enough height to perform this mount.
4. Initially, have the participants perform the straddle position on the beam just to experience the correct balance point.
5. Initially, have the participants practice jumping up, raising the hips and straddling the legs. When sufficient height is reached, attempt to place feet up on the beam in a straddle position. Repeat several times.

Spotting
1. Stand on the opposite side of the beam from the gymnast and place hands on her upper arms. Assist the gymnast in maintaining balance and keep her from tumbling forward.
2. Spotter must be prepared for any sudden falls by positioning her body in a secure stance.

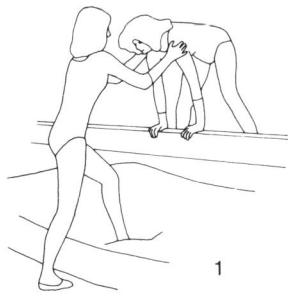

1

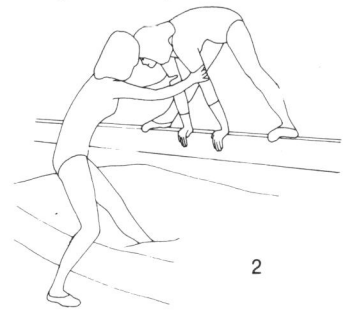

2

SKILL	DESCRIPTION	TEACHING TECHNIQUES AND OBSERVATION POINTS
12. Lunge 	The lunge is a very easy, static position for most girls. The lunge may be performed in a forward or sideways position. See illustrations for the body positions. 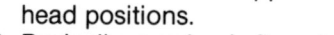	1. Allow students the opportunity to create their own arm and head positions. 2. Basically, one leg is flexed and the other is fully extended at the knee, ankle or both. *Spotting* 1. The spotter should stand to the side of the beam with arms extended.
13. Changement	1. Begin with feet in fifth position with the right foot in front. 2. Bend the knees and spring upward, landing in fifth position with the left foot in front, arms lateral.	1. Gymnasts must be able to spring high enough to allow the ankle to extend fully before landing again. 2. Keep eyes on the beam. 3. Allow the knees to bend slightly when landing. 4. Keep legs close together. *Spotting* 1. The spotter should stand beside the beam with arms outstretched.
14. Tuck Jump 	1. Begin with one foot ahead of the other. Bend the knees, lifting the heels from the beam. 2. Spring upward, raising the knees up towards the chest. Quickly extend the legs and flex them slightly as the feet contact the beam in the landing.	1. Keep legs close together. 2. Maintain excellent posture. 3. Arms are best kept low and close to the body. However, some participants may find it necessary to use the arms to turn the body. 4. Turn must be performed on the balls of the foot. 5. Turn toward the rear foot. *Spotting* 1. The spotter should stand beside the beam with arms extended.
15. One-half Turn on Toes of One Foot	See description of Turns on One Foot (page 30) in Floor Exercise section.	1. Body alignment is essential. Head is held up and shoulders relaxed. 2. The turn is executed high on the ball of the foot. *Spotting* 1. Stand beside the beam, arms extended.

| SKILL | DESCRIPTION | TEACHING TECHNIQUES AND OBSERVATION POINTS |

16. Squat Turn

1. Begin in a deep squat position, on the toes, one foot in front of the other.
2. Pivot one-half turn on balls of the feet.

1. Keep knees close together.
2. Back should be straight, head up.
3. Arms may be out at sides or held low and close to the body.

Spotting
1. The spotter should stand beside the beam with arms extended.

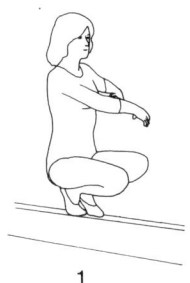
1

2

3

17. Back Shoulder Roll (rolling over right shoulder)

1. Lie on the beam face up. Place head to side so the right shoulder is on the beam.
2. Reach with the hands over the head to place right hand under beam, left hand on top of the beam.
3. Lift legs to chest, rolling on right shoulder to place the right knee on the beam.
4. Shift the right hand to the top of the beam, extend both arms and lift the head and torso to the knee scale position.

1. Keep legs close to the chest in a tuck or pike position.
2. Use the right hand under the beam to help pull the legs over the shoulder.
3. Remember to change the right hand to the top of the beam to help take the weight off the shoulder.
4. Have the gymnast put the right knee close to the forehead.

Spotting
1. Initially, use two spotters, one on either side of the beam.
2. Stand close to the beam, beside the gymnast's waist.
3. As her legs are raised and her hips pass over her head, grasp her hips with both hands, and lift them until her knee is on the beam.
4. Steady the gymnast until her head is in the final position.

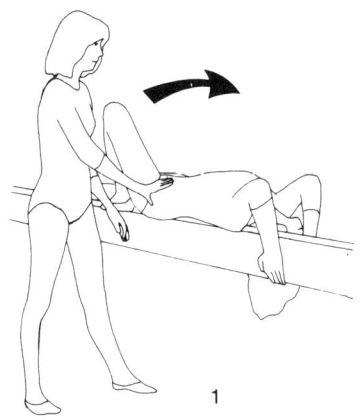
1
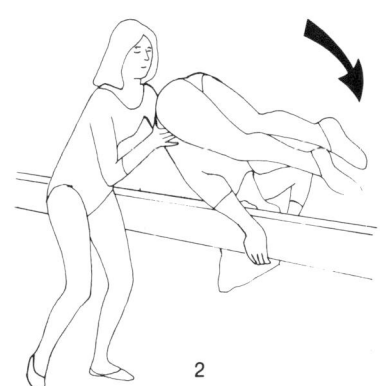
2
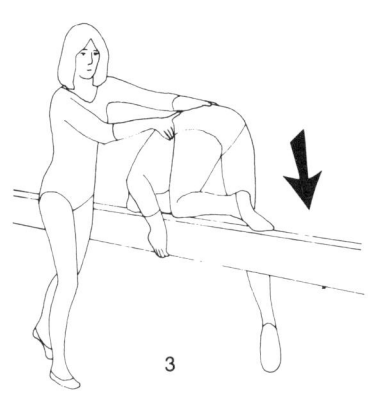
3

69

SKILL	DESCRIPTION	TEACHING TECHNIQUES AND OBSERVATION POINTS
18. Straddle Jump Dismount	As for the straight jump dismount, but raise the legs to a horizontal position in a wide straddle.	1. See straight jump dismount, page 66. 2. Keep back straight, head up. *Spotting* 1. See straight jump dismount.

1

2

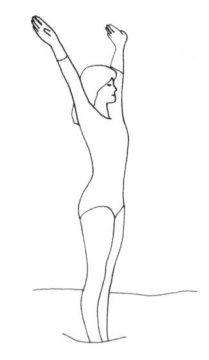

3

Level III Skills

19. Squat Mount	1. Stand facing the beam, with hands on the beam approximately shoulder width apart. 2. Jump to support, keeping the arms straight. 3. Lift knees to chest, placing the balls of the feet on the beam, between the hands. 4. Keep the hips low and the head up.	1. As in the straddle mount, the gymnast must allow the shoulders to come forward of the hand position. Initially, gymnasts may wish to get into a deep squat position on the beam to experience this balance point. 2. Arms must be straight throughout. 3. Gymnasts must first think of jumping up and *then* onto the beam. To assist the gymnast, lower the beam in the early stages of this movement. 4. Gymnasts must be able to perform a deep squat position, otherwise this element will be difficult. 5. Do not lower the heels, but remain on the balls of the feet. 6. Hips must be kept low when squatting. 7. Some gymnasts may wish to use a beat board.

1

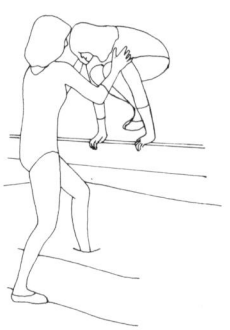

2

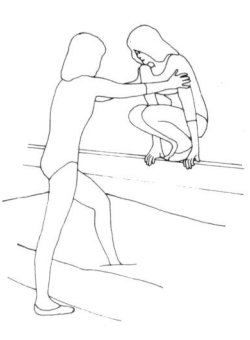

3

Spotting
1. Stand on the opposite side of the beam from the gymnast and support her by the upper arms.
2. Do not *pull* the gymnast into position.
3. For those gymnasts having difficulty, a second spotter may stand on the same side as the gymnast and assist with the squatting action by lifting by the back of her upper leg while grasping her upper arm.

SKILL	DESCRIPTION	TEACHING TECHNIQUES AND OBSERVATION POINTS

20. Single Leg Mount to Squat Position

1. Approaching the beam from an angle, reach for the beam with the inside hand. As the hand grips the beam, quickly swing the inside leg forward and upward to place the foot on the beam ahead of the hand.
2. As the hand leaves the beam, the second foot follows the first to be placed on the beam, slightly ahead of the first. The performer remains in a squat position, arms free.

1. This mount requires a one-foot take off. Performers should practice the run-up and the take off before actually attempting the entire mount.
2. A beat board is usually used with this mount. Placement of the beat board is almost parallel to the beam.
3. Lower the beam to a comfortable height.
4. Gymnasts must lean into the jump to keep their momentum going forward.
5. Hold the squat position until balance is attained.
6. As the gymnast becomes more proficient in performing this mount, she may wish to attempt it without using the hand. Gymnasts may also wish to land in an upright position, rather than a squat.
7. Watch for slippery footwear.

Spotting
1. Stand beside the gymnast holding the *hand* and the *upper arm* of her outside arm. Run to the beam with her, lifting her as she steps onto the beam. Steady her in the squat position.
2. An additional spotter may stand on the opposite side of the beam, ready to grasp the *upper part* of the gymnast's inside arm that is placed on the beam.

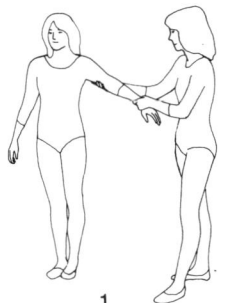 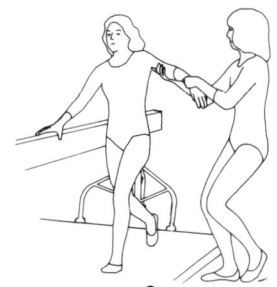 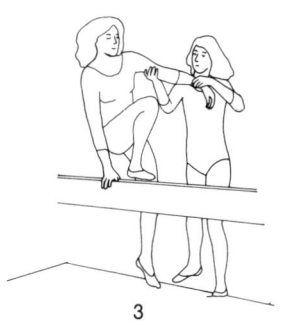 

1   2   3   4

21. Bent Knee Pose

Please see illustration.

1. This is a static pose and the arm and head positions are optional.
2. Keep the knees together.
3. The back should be slightly arched.

Spotting
1. The spotter should stand beside the beam with arms extended.

SKILL	DESCRIPTION	TEACHING TECHNIQUES AND OBSERVATION POINTS
22. Arabesque 	1. Stand on the right leg and raise the left leg to the rear as high as possible, bending the trunk forward. 2. Hold the head up. Arm positions may vary.	1. This is a balance position and demands a considerable amount of control. Gymnasts must move into and out of this position slowly. 2. Instructors may wish to allow a variety of leg and trunk positions to accommodate the ability levels of the gymnasts. 3. Legs must be straight and the foot pointed. 4. Have the gymnast begin by raising her leg only slightly. As control is increased, she can raise the leg higher and bend the trunk forward. 5. Gymnasts may wish to try various methods of moving into and out of this position. *Spotting* 1. Take the gymnast's hand and assist her to the correct balance point.
23. Sissone	See Floor Exercise, Level III.	1. Keep the eyes on the beam during the landing. 2. Initially, do not attempt to jump too high. 3. This movement should be as smooth as possible. *Spotting* 1. Move with the performer, alongside the beam. Extend a hand in case the gymnast requires assistance in maintaining her balance.
24. Scissors Leap	See Floor Exercise, Level III Routine.	1. Gymnasts may find it easier to precede this leap with a step. Step left to initiate leap with the right leg. 2. Do not attempt to raise legs too high in the early stages of learning this skill. 3. Keep eyes on the beam during landing. Keep the head up. *Spotting* 1. Stand alongside the beam with hand extended to the performer.
25. Kick Turn	1. This skill is usually preceded by a step. Step left, kick the right leg forward and upward. Rotate the body to the left and pivot on the ball of the left foot, making a half turn.	1. Keep the shoulders directly over the left foot throughout the movement. Balance will be more easily maintained. Arch the back slightly to achieve this. 2. The turn must be executed on the toes. 3. Legs are straight, feet pointed. 4. In the early stages, do not attempt to kick the right leg too high.

1

2

3

SKILL	DESCRIPTION	TEACHING TECHNIQUES AND OBSERVATION POINTS
	2. End in an arabesque or move immediately into a locomotor skill. 3. Arm positions are optional. A suggested arm movement is from the sides of the body to above the head, arms rounded. 4. The eyes should watch the end of the beam.	*Spotting* 1. The spotter should stand beside the beam with arms extended.
26. Forward Roll	1. See Forward Roll with Spotting, page 65.	1. Gymnasts should be prepared to attempt the forward roll without spotting by the time Level III is reached. Progress should be gradual. Spotting should be continued as the gymnast becomes more proficient, slowly easing up on the amount of support and assistance. 2. Instructors must realize that abilities will vary, and that the withdrawal of spotter support should be tailored to the need of each gymnast.
27. Backward Roll	1. From a balanced back lying or supine position on the beam, place the thumbs on top of the beam under the neck, the fingers gripping the sides of the beam. 2. Raise the legs over the head. As this position is reached, extend the arms to take the weight off the shoulders. 3. Place the foot or the knee on the beam to finish in a squat or knee scale position. 4. Lift the head and focus on the end of the beam.	1. Some gymnasts will find it difficult to raise their legs in a pike position over the head. In this case a tuck position may be used. 2. Keep the elbows close to the head for support. 3. Keep in mind that the knees should be close to the forehead when landing out of the roll. This helps to keep the gymnast oriented. *Spotting* See spotting for back shoulder roll, page 69.

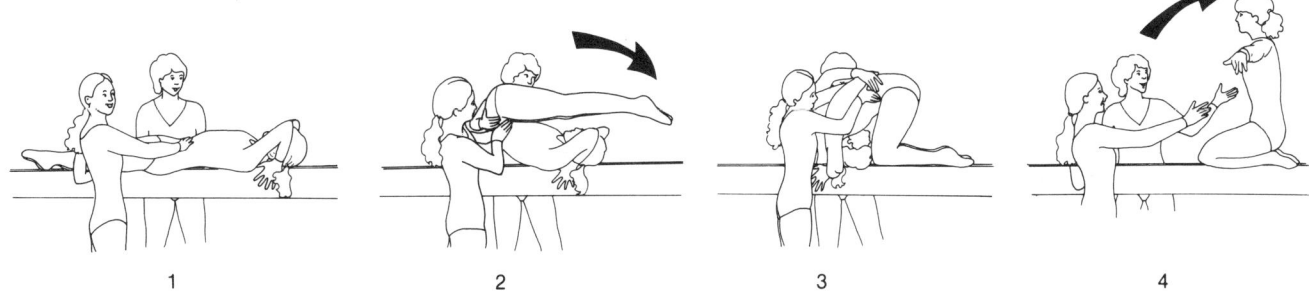

1 2 3 4

SKILL	DESCRIPTION	TEACHING TECHNIQUES AND OBSERVATION POINTS

28. Round-Off Dismount (off the end of the beam)	1. Begin about 80 centimeters (2½′) from the end of the beam. Lift the right leg upward, raising the arms overhead.
	2. As the right leg is lowered to take the weight, place both hands together across the width of the beam (fingers along the edge), while kicking the left leg, then the right to a side handstand.
	3. Hold the handstand momentarily and push off the beam, executing a quarter turn.
	4. Land, facing the end of the beam.
		1. Initially gymnasts will pike at the hips to allow the feet to land on the mat. Attempt to keep the body straight all the way to the landing. This can be attained by:
		  a) pushing with the shoulders and wrists after the feet have passed the inverted position;
		  b) lifting the chest so the body is vertical before the feet contact the mat.
		2. Keep arms straight.
		3. Reach the handstand position before initiating the quarter turn.
		4. The gymnast must be able to perform a round-off on the floor before attempting this skill.
		5. Practice on a Swedish box is helpful.
		6. The higher the beam, the easier it is to prepare for landing.
		
		Spotting
		1. Stand at the end of the beam, to the back of the gymnast. As the gymnast places her hands on the beam, grasp her upper arm.
		2. After the gymnast executes her quarter turn and is preparing to land, the spotter places her other hand on the gymnast's hip to assist the performer with a straight body landing.
		3. The spotter should keep a hand on the performer until she has control of the landing.

 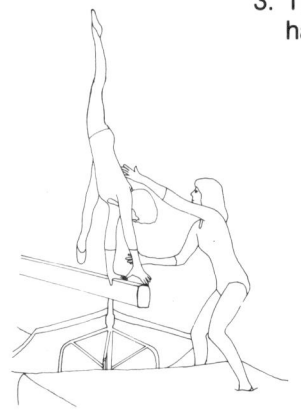 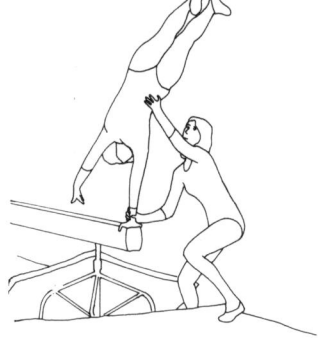 

1   2   3   4

SKILL	DESCRIPTION	TEACHING TECHNIQUES AND OBSERVATION POINTS
29. Routine	1. Squat mount (mount beam to right of middle) 2. Stand 3. Bent knee pose 4. Quarter turn to left 5. Three backward steps to end of beam 6. Stretch on toes 7. Arabesque (attitude) 8. Front scale	1. The Level III routine incorporates skills from the previous two levels as well as some taught in the Level III unit. The idea is to have the gymnasts learn to perform a specific set of skills and to perform them in such a way that the routine flows from one skill to the next. The routine involves dance movements as well as tumbling skills. Execution should be stressed. 2. It is best for all arm movements to be optional with suggestions and guidance coming from the instructor. 3. If there is a Level IV student available, it is helpful if she demonstrates the routine in its entirety first. Then break it down into beam lengths and present it in that manner.

| SKILL | DESCRIPTION | TEACHING TECHNIQUES AND OBSERVATION POINTS |

9. Chassé (step-together-step)
10. High kick to front lunge position
11. Jump to squat position (back leg in lunge position leads)
12. Squat turn (to face opposite direction)
13. Tuck jump with height
14. Forward roll (support)
15. V-sit
16. Swing legs down and back (straddling beam) to knee scale
17. Stand quarter turn
18. Tuck jump dismount

4. Stress form, grace and poise. Look for height on the chassé, high kick, tuck jump, and dismount.
5. Be sure the gymnasts realize that the routine must be memorized.
6. Teach the routine to the entire group on the floor first.

Level IV Skills

30. Step On End Mount

1. Face the end of the beam. Place the beat board at right angles to the end of the beam.
2. From a running approach, using a one-foot take off, spring vertically up to step with the other foot onto the end of the beam.
3. The hands do not touch the beam at all.
4. The landing is in an upright position.

1. See Level III, single leg mount to squat position, page 71.
2. Lift from the lead leg and push from the trailing leg.
3. Keep eyes on the end of the beam for correct foot placement.
4. Some gymnasts may prefer to assume a squat position rather than an upright position upon landing on the beam.

Spotting
As for the single leg mount to squat position.

1

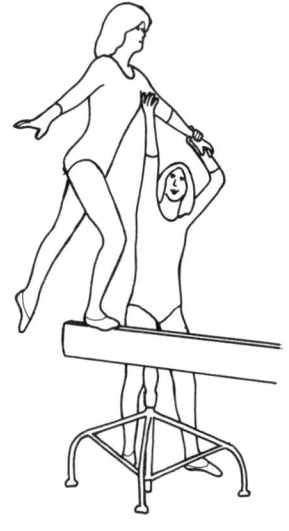

2

SKILL	DESCRIPTION	TEACHING TECHNIQUES AND OBSERVATION POINTS

31. Forward Roll Mount

1. Place the beat board at the end of the beam.
2. From a run, jump, placing hands on either side of the beam.

1. Some gymnasts may be unable to roll smoothly to an upright position. These performers should be encouraged to lower their hands under the beam and stop momentarily as their hips are lowered to the beam. If their roll is slightly crooked, this allows them to adjust the hips, so they may continue the roll to a stand without falling off.
2. Practice on a Swedish box is helpful.

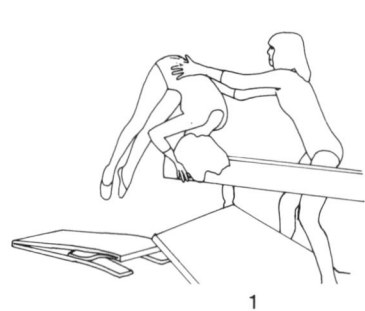
1

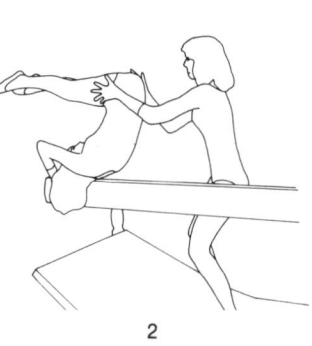
2

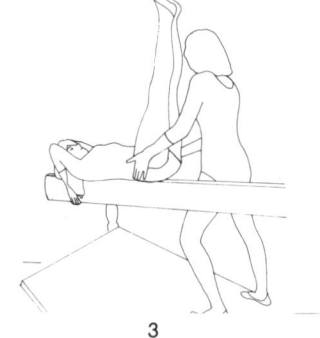
3

3. With arms straight, lift the hips high, then bend the arms, tuck head and perform a forward roll.

3. A padded beam (towels may be used) is also useful in the initial stages.
4. Review the techniques of the forward roll on the beam (see page 65).
5. The gymnast must control the roll.

Spotting
1. See the spotting for the forward roll with spotting (page 65).
2. An additional spotter may be used to lift the gymnast's legs as they leave the beat board. This provides the gymnast with assistance in controlling the roll.

32. Splits

1. Begin by facing the length of the beam, one foot ahead of the other.
2. Slide the front leg forward and the back leg backward.
3. With control, slide down to a split on the beam. Arm position is optional.

1. See discussion of splits technique in Appendix III.
2. Splits may be performed with manual support. From a deep lunge position, reach down with both hands to grasp the beam. Lower legs to split position.

Spotting
1. Stand beside gymnast, holding her hand until a balanced position is reached.

1

2

33. Split Leap

See Split Leap (page 34) in the Floor Exercise section.

SKILL	DESCRIPTION	TEACHING TECHNIQUES AND OBSERVATION POINTS
34. Full Turn	See Turns on One Foot (page 30) in the Floor Exercise section. See also discussion of turns under Dance (page 19).	
35. Continuous Forward Roll	1. Perform the forward roll as described on page 65. 2. Do not stop the momentum, but continue the roll to a stand.	1. Once this skill is perfected, there is no need to grasp the underside of the beam. 2. Progress from a starting position in a squat to a deep lunge. 3. Do not roll too fast. 4. Keep the body rounded. 5. Practice on a Swedish box is useful. *Spotting* 1. As described for the forward roll (see page 65). 2. Spotter must be ready to move to the side, to get out of the way of the legs lowering to the beam.

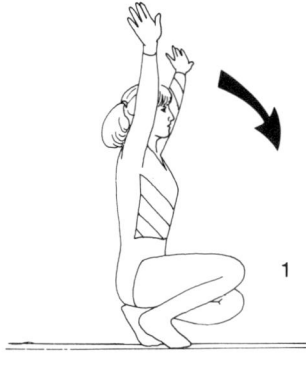  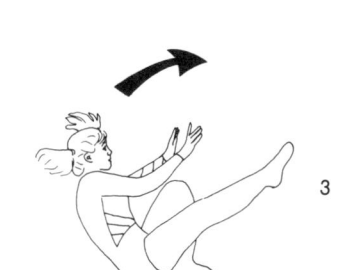 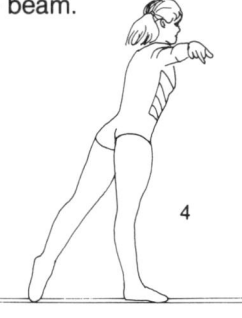

36. Cartwheel	1. This is performed as on the floor (see page 28), with a few changes. 2. A completely lateral cartwheel is difficult to perform so a cartwheel, quarter-turn inward, is usually done.	1. As in all balance beam skills, practice on the floor is essential. Each gymnast must move through the progressions—line on the floor, bench, low beam, high beam. 2. The legs and arms are kept straight, except when taking off and landing. 3. The landing leg is placed closer to the hand in the early stages of learning.

SKILL	DESCRIPTION	TEACHING TECHNIQUES AND OBSERVATION POINTS
	4. Attempt to raise the upper body as soon as the landing foot makes contact with the beam. 5. In beginning stages, gymnasts may find it easier to place hands close together.	*Spotting* 1. The spotter should stand beside the beam, using a raised platform to reach the performer. 2. The gymnast should be spotted with both hands at her hips. 3. The spotter should keep the gymnast from falling off the beam. 4. It is important for the spotter to maintain contact until the gymnast is steady. 5. The spotter should assist with the rhythm.
37. Front Walkover	1. This is performed the same way as a front walkover on the floor (see page 37). 2. From a standing position, arms raised over the head, lean forward to place the hands on either side of the beam, thumbs meeting on the top. 3. Kick one leg over, then the other, splitting the legs in the inverted position. The gymnast should be watching the beam to see her lead foot as it makes contact with the beam. 4. The weight is transferred over the foot, and abdominal strength and momentum bring the body to the upright position.	1. This skill requires considerable flexibility to enable the gymnast to see her lead foot land on the beam. 2. Practice and preparation using all progressions is essential. 3. Shoulders and hips must be square throughout. 4. The movement is done fairly quickly without pausing on the hands. 5. Piling mats up until they are even with the height of the beam will remove some of the fear factor for the gymnast. *Spotting* 1. Good preparation, prior to the performance on the high beam, makes the job of the spotter much easier. 2. Initially, two or three spotters should be used. One should check to see that the lead foot is securely placed on the beam. The other two should assist the gymnast to an upright position and provide support. 3. Spotters may stand on a raised platform if necessary. 4. Hand placement is as for the walkover on the floor (see page 37). 5. Do not lift the gymnast. Allow her to take her weight on the beam.

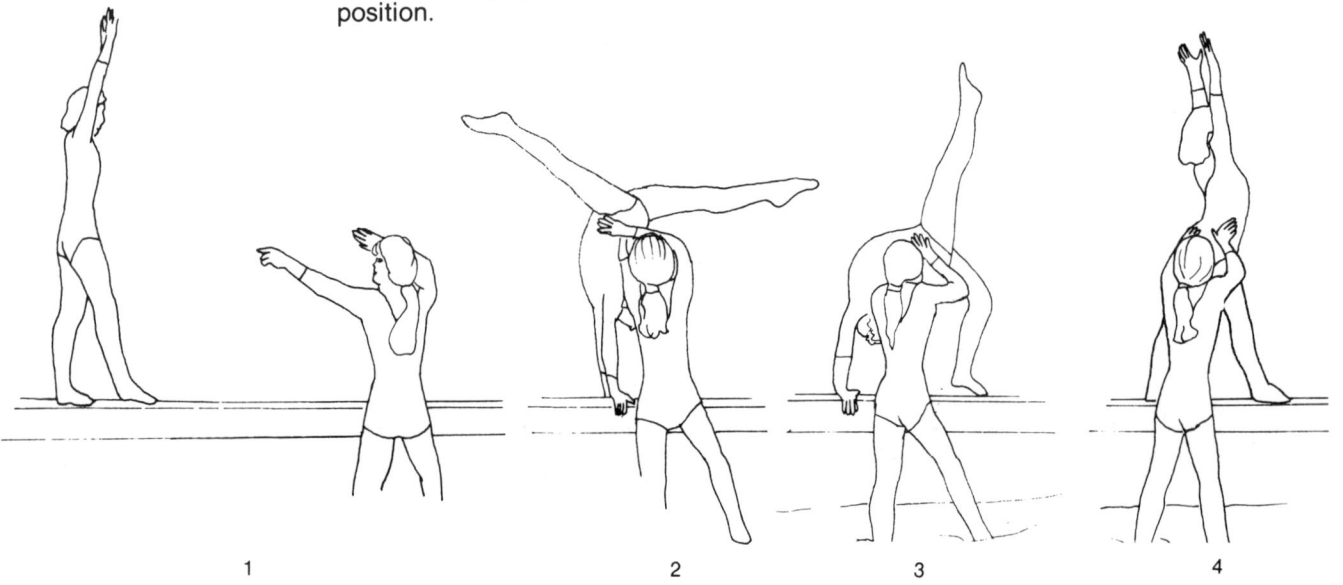

1 2 3 4

SKILL	DESCRIPTION	TEACHING TECHNIQUES AND OBSERVATION POINTS
38. Back Walkover	1. This is performed the same way as a back walkover on the floor (see page 38). 2. Begin in a standing position with one foot ahead of the other and weight on the back foot. Arms should be raised, shoulders stretched, shoulders and hips square. 3. The arms precede the head as the upper body moves backward. As the hands contact the beam, (hand placement is as for the front walkover) the last foot pushes off. 4. The legs are split in the inverted position.	1. Progress slowly, learning the movement well before proceeding to the next stage. 2. The movement is performed fairly quickly. 3. Finish the skill in a lunge or an arabesque. *Spotting* 1. The spotter stands with her back to the gymnast with arms raised ready to grasp the gymnast's hips. Thumbs point toward each other, and fingers reach around the outside of the hips. 2. The spotter must first check to see that the gymnast places her hands correctly and securely on the beam. 3. The spotter must not lift the gymnast, but guide her and assist her in reaching the handstand position. 4. Very often the crucial moment is as the gymnast prepares to lean backwards. Spotters must be prepared to give support at this time.

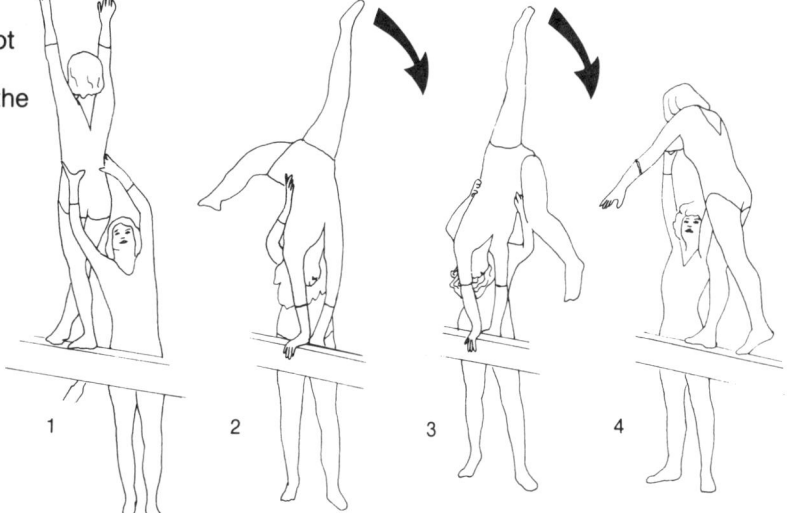

39. Optional Routine	Design a routine using skills appropriate to the gymnast's ability. The routine should be no less than three full lengths.	1. When designing a balance beam routine, one must consider the following:
		   a) The complete length of the beam should be used.
		   b) Perform at a variety of levels i.e., high and low.
		   c) Turns, jumps and leaps must be included.
		   d) Include rhythm changes.
		   e) Tumbling skills should be distributed throughout the routine.
		   f) The routine should begin with a mount and end with a dismount.
		   g) Do not repeat skills.
		2. Balance should be stressed. Gymnasts should keep falls to a minimum.
		3. Some students may have difficulty getting their routine started. Allow them to use the Level III routine and change various skills to ones more appropriate to their ability or preference.
		4. Have the students practice their judging on each other's routines.
		5. The routine should be performed without pauses. Stress correct form.

D. Vault

Many secondary school girls are afraid of vaulting, and many of them will never succeed in mastering this skill. It is important, therefore, not to force a student to perform a progression before *she* feels she is ready. Instead, give her very close spotting and tremendous amounts of encouragement to build up her confidence. She will then be able to relax and attend to the techniques of performing a vault.

Vaulting can be divided into seven distinct phases (CGF LEVEL III). The seven parts are:
- The Run
- The Hurdle
- The Take off
- The Pre-flight
- The Push off
- The Post-flight
- The Landing

Vaults at the classroom level rarely show these seven parts distinctly. Simple vaults do, however, require a long run to build up momentum and a strong spring from the beat board to enable the participant to get through the vault. Contact is directly on top of the horse and for a split second only. The post-flight should take the gymnast some distance from the horse and the landing must be smooth and controlled.

General Safety

1. A double thickness of mats should be provided for landings. A crash pad is recommended.
2. Additional mats should be placed to allow for a vault that goes off to one side, or for vaults that over-rotate on landing.
3. Do not overlap mats. If mats tend to slide, use tape to hold them together.
4. Be sure the vaulting horse is stable. It should be secured to the floor for difficult vaults. The holes from the pommels should be covered with tape so fingers will not slip into them.
5. If a Swedish box is to be used, be sure all sections are properly in place and secure.
6. Slippery footwear should not be worn. A light slipper with a thin rubber sole is the most effective footwear for vaulting.
7. Keep the run-up to the vault clear at all times. Be sure it is clearly marked so other gymnasts do not wander into the path of the approaching vaulter.
8. It is recommended that only a beat board be used for take-off apparatus. If two beat boards are available, placing one on top of the other provides additional spring and height.
9. Set all vaulting apparatus as low as necessary to accommodate the height and ability of the gymnast comfortably. The type of vault being performed must also be considered when setting the height of the horse.
10. Do not allow gymnasts to vault without a spotter. The gymnast must notify the spotter of the vault she intends to perform.
11. The gymnast must be properly warmed up before vaulting. Particular attention must be paid to warm-up exercises for the shoulders, back, and ankles.
12. Shin splints, where there is an ache in the shin area, is a common injury in vaulting. Knee socks to keep the legs warm, and padding in the shoes help to avoid this injury. A runway that is too hard will also cause shin splints.
13. The performer should learn the proper run, take off and landing before learning the specific vaults.

Teaching Techniques Common to all Vaults

i. Using the Beat Board

The beat board is also known as the reuther board. If it is to be used, proper preparation and instruction in its use must be undertaken by the instructor. The following points should be noted.

1. The most flexible section of the board begins approximately 30 cm (1') behind the forward edge of the board. It is important that the top of the toes touch the board in this area to give the gymnast the maximum lift. After the toes touch the board, the heels also come down momentarily. Circle the most flexible area of the board with chalk so the gymnasts can easily see it.
2. All vaults require a two-foot take off from the beat board. To practice this, have the students take two or three walking steps, swing one leg forward and up, land on both feet, and immediately spring off with both feet. The arms swing backward as the feet land, and forward to shoulder level on the take off.

    Repeat the above movement using the beat board and a mat.

    Emphasize a low, fast hurdle. For the take off, the hip, knee and ankle joint are flexed only slightly and then quickly extended to get a good upward thrust from the beat board.
3. As the participants become more comfortable with the hurdle and the two-foot take off, have them perform it using a longer run.
4. The distance the beat board is from the horse depends on the individual and the vault she is doing. Beginner gymnasts will want to place the board right up next to the horse. Encourage them to work with it at least 30 cm (1') away from the vaulting horse.

    As the speed of the run is increased, and the take off perfected, the beat board will just naturally be moved back to allow the gymnast the pre-flight she will require. For layout vaults, the beat board must be at least body length from the vaulting horse.
5. Serious vaulters will require in-depth coaching to allow them to progress to more difficult vaults. For these gymnasts, it is recommended that instructors refer to the C.G.F. *Coaching Certification Manual Level II*.

ii. The Run

For the serious gymnast, the run is one of the most important aspects of the vault. The running technique is much the same as that used in sprinting or the approach to the long jump. The gymnast should be encouraged to begin slowly, and gradually increase speed so as to reach a maximum speed three or four meters (9-12') before the hurdle. The following additional points concerning the run should be considered:

1. The gymnast should try to be consistent in her run, hurdle, and take off. To achieve this, she may wish to measure her approach distance and mark the starting point. She should also begin her run with the same foot, so that her hurdle becomes familiar and consistent.
2. Instructors should draw the gymnast's attention to the use of the arms in the run. Good running techniques should be discussed.

iii. Pre- and Post-flight

1. Vaults demonstrating good pre- and post-flight are not commonly seen in the school gymnastics program. They require considerable time and practice.
2. In the pre-flight for the basic vaults (squat, straddle, and stoop) the body should be at least horizontal at the moment the hands contact the vaulting horse. In layout vaults, the body should be 45° above the horizontal in the pre-flight. According to the Canadian Gymnastics Federation, the angle of the body is dependent upon the speed of the run, the type of vault being performed, and the amount of push off from the horse.
3. Post-flight should always be as long and as high as possible.

iv. Push Off

1. The ideal push off from the horse is achieved by placing the hands ahead of the shoulders when contacting the horse. The hands are shoulder width apart and placed on top of the horse in the middle.
2. The touch of the hands on the horse should be as short as possible. The push comes from the hands, and the extension of the arms and shoulders.

v. Landing

1. Gymnasts should be expected to demonstrate a *controlled landing* out of all vaults and dismounts. The landing is first made on the toes, the heels are then lowered, and the knees and hips flex to absorb the impact.
2. Gymnasts should get into the habit of counting to three after each vault. This helps to remind them to finish the vault correctly.
3. Practice correct landings by jumping off various heights and demonstrate controlled landings.

| SKILL | DESCRIPTION | TEACHING TECHNIQUES AND OBSERVATION POINTS |

Level I Skills

1. Squat Vault

1. After the take off, extend the body, reaching with the hands for the horse. Then flex the hips, bringing the knees to the chest above the horse.
2. Immediately push off with the hands, lifting the head and chest upward. Extend the body in the air and land with knees bent.

1

2

1. Use the following teaching progressions:
   a) Run, jump, and place hands on horse.
   b) Run, jump to squat on the horse, stand, jump to a full extension in the air, control landing.
2. Use a variety of heights depending on the abilities of the gymnasts.
3. Some gymnasts may attempt "to hop through the arms." Remind gymnasts that the hands are on the horse only momentarily. Practice the push-off section by standing in front of a wall with extended arms. Fall toward the wall, then push off as quickly as possible. Extend the shoulders and wrists. Elbows should be locked. Remind gymnasts to use the fingers for a final push.
4. Keep the head up to avoid tumbling forward.
5. Gymnasts will progress at different rates. Stress perfecting each skill before moving to the next progression.
6. To practice moving from an extended position to a tuck position, begin in a fully extended push-up position on the floor. As quickly as possible, pull the knees to a squat position, then return to the extended position. Then practice coming from the extended position to a squat and then to a stand.
7. Some performers, due to their size or lack of flexibility, will be unable to assume a squat position without some difficulty. Ask all gymnasts to demonstrate a squat position on the floor in order to determine which ones will require special assistance.
8. The instructor will be able to identify those who react negatively to the vault by spotting each gymnast in her first attempts. These gymnasts may require a modified vaulting program. Please see page 97 for some suggestions on modified progressions.

Spotting
1. Use two spotters at all times, one on either side of the gymnast.
2. Stand on the *far side* of the horse and watch the performer's hands as she contacts the horse. Grasp her wrists with the nearest hand and her upper arm with the other hand.
3. Move with the gymnast as she travels over the horse and lands.
4. Be sure she has controlled her landing before releasing your grip.

| SKILL | DESCRIPTION | TEACHING TECHNIQUES AND OBSERVATION POINTS |

Level II Skills

2. Straddle Vault

1. After the take off, extend the body. As the hands contact the horse, quickly bend the hips, bringing the legs sideways in a wide straddle.
2. Travel over the horse in a straddle, pushing off with the hands. Extend the body in the air, and bring the legs together before the landing.

1. Use the following teaching progressions:
   a) Begin on the floor in a fully extended push-up position (front support position). Push with the hands, moving the legs to a straddle position. Attempt to place the feet ahead of where the hands were.
   b) Run, straddle on top of the vaulting horse.
   c) Practice vaulting a straddle position with the horse set at various heights. The Swedish box is very useful for this purpose.
2. This movement requires hip flexibility in the straddle position.
3. Be sure hips are high and legs wide enough to clear the horse.
4. Keep the head up.
5. Legs must be straight, and feet pointed.

Spotting
1. Stand on the far side of the horse, facing the performer. Stand with one foot ahead of the other, ready to step back as the gymnast travels over the horse. Grasp the performer's upper arms and move backwards with her until she has controlled her landing.
2. A gymnast may find it difficult to understand how she can land when the spotter is so close to the horse. Assure her you will move in time.
3. Be prepared for the gymnast who does not hold her head up. Keep your head back in this case.

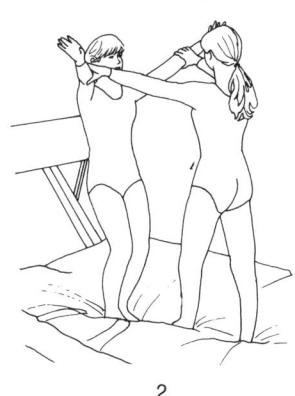

Level III Skills

The skills involved in Levels III and IV are for advanced gymnasts only. Instructors should refer to the C.G.F. *Coaching Certification Manual Level II.*

3. Layout Squat

1. The layout position involves lifting the body to a position 25° - 45° above the horizontal, before the hands contact the horse.

1. Proper preparation is *essential* to performing this skill.
2. The beat board must be at least one body length from the vaulting horse.
3. A layout vault requires a considerable amount of practice. Do not rush the progression. Each stage of the vault must be perfected.

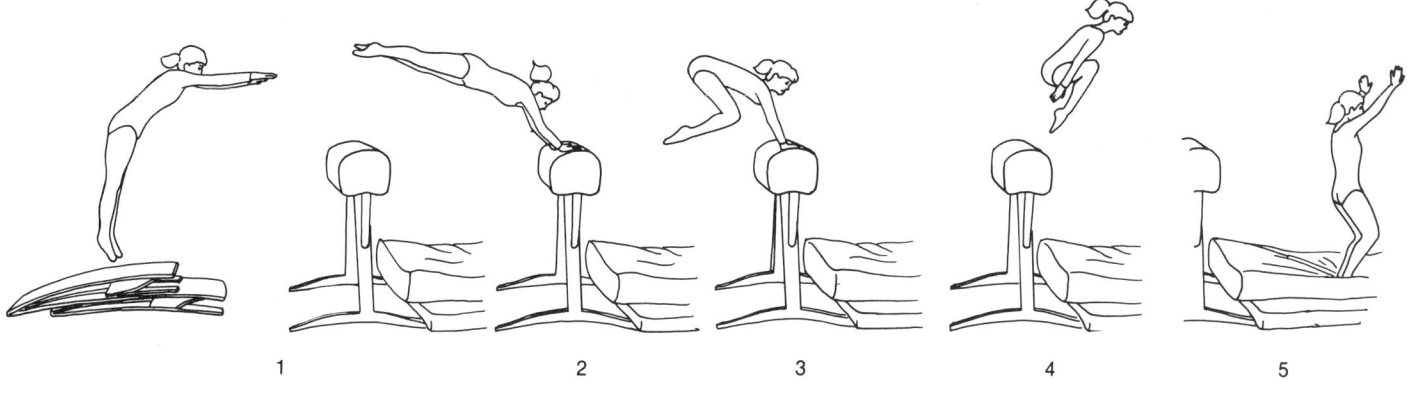

SKILL	DESCRIPTION	TEACHING TECHNIQUES AND OBSERVATION POINTS
	2. From this layout position, tuck the knees to the chest, at the same time pushing with the hands so the upper body is lifted. 3. Extend the body before landing.	*Spotting* 1. Use as many as four spotters. 2. Two on the near side of the horse assist with the layout position by lifting the gymnast's upper thigh and abdomen. 3. Two on the far side of the horse grasp the upper arms and assist the gymnast to clear the horse and control her landing.

Level IV Skills

4. Layout Straddle Vault

1. From the layout position, swing the legs to the side and straddle over the horse.
2. Push hard with the hands and lift the upper body.
3. Bring legs together and extend body in the air before landing.

1. Refer to the straddle vault and the layout squat (page 83).
2. Do not straddle legs until after the layout position is achieved.
3. Legs should be straight and feet pointed throughout.

Spotting
1. See straddle vault (page 83).

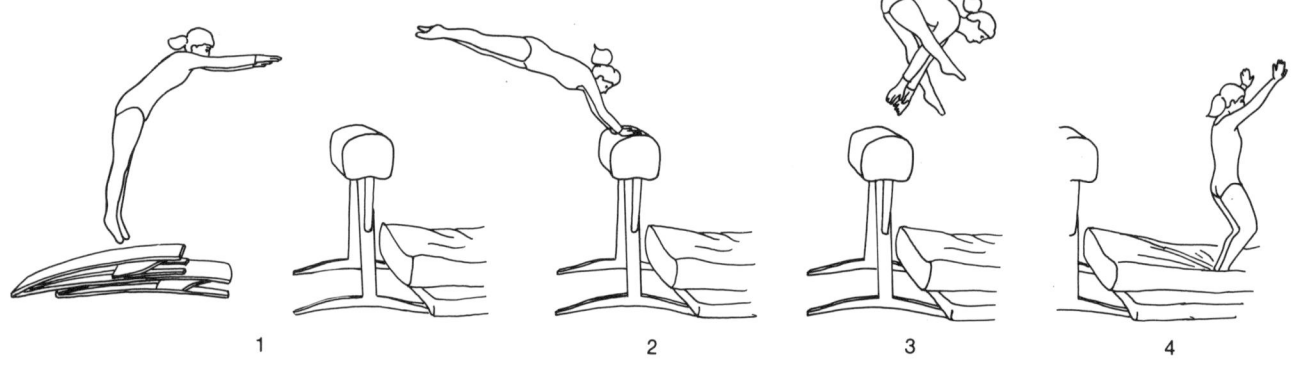

5. Stoop Vault

1. After the take off, extend the body and reach for the horse.

1. Many gymnasts find this a difficult vault to perform. It requires good hip flexibility.
2. Push the hips forward to allow the body to extend before landing.

 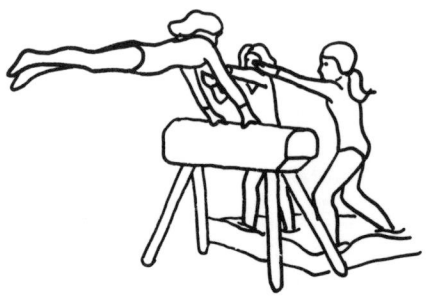 

SKILL	DESCRIPTION	TEACHING TECHNIQUES AND OBSERVATIONS

2. As the hands contact the horse, flex the hips and move the legs downward and forward. The legs must be straight and together, with the body in a pike position as it travels over the horse.
3. A good, strong push off with the hands and shoulders is required, so the legs will clear the horse.

3. Arms and legs are straight throughout the skill.
4. Some gymnasts will be nervous about catching their feet on the horse. A strong push-off stage is required.

Spotting
1. See squat vault (page 82).

6. Handspring

1. From the layout position, the straight body must travel upward, past 45° above the horizontal, before the hands contact the horse.
2. As the body passes through the handstand position on the horse, there is a strong push off to obtain maximum post-flight.
3. The body remains straight throughout the skill, until the landing, when the hips and knees flex as the toes come in contact with the mat.

1. A handspring is a difficult vault to develop, but it is basic to more complicated vaults. It usually takes two to three years to perfect a handspring.
2. Well-learned basics are the pre-requisite to this skill.
3. Use the following teaching progressions:
   a) Handspring with two-foot landings on the floor.
   b) Kick to a handstand and fall with a straight body onto a crash pad.
   c) From a Swedish box, perform front handspring onto mats. Use two spotters.
   d) Place a trampoline with a crash pad on top, up against the landing side of the horse. A spotter stands between the beat board and the horse and lifts the gymnast to the handstand position on the horse. As the gymnast leaves the beat board from her run, she must maintain a straight, controlled body while being assisted by the spotter. The gymnast lands on the crash pad as described in b).

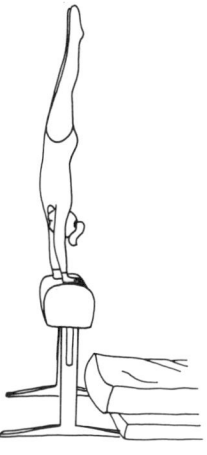

1

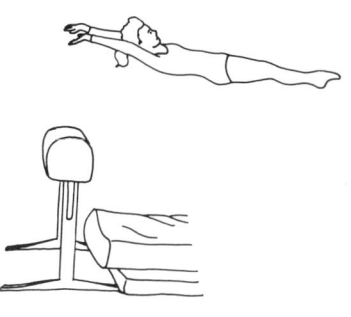

2

SKILL	DESCRIPTION	TEACHING TECHNIQUES AND OBSERVATION POINTS

　　　e) Handspring with three spotters. One spotter assists on the pre-flight, as for the other layout vaults, and the other two assist on the post-flight. Spotters grasp the gymnast's upper arms with both hands and carry the gymnast through to the landing.
3. The handspring has a very even rhythm. The pre-flight and post-flight are very similar in distance and height.
4. The arms are straight throughout the vault.
5. The head is between the arms or slightly tilted forward on the chest.

Spotting
　　As described above.

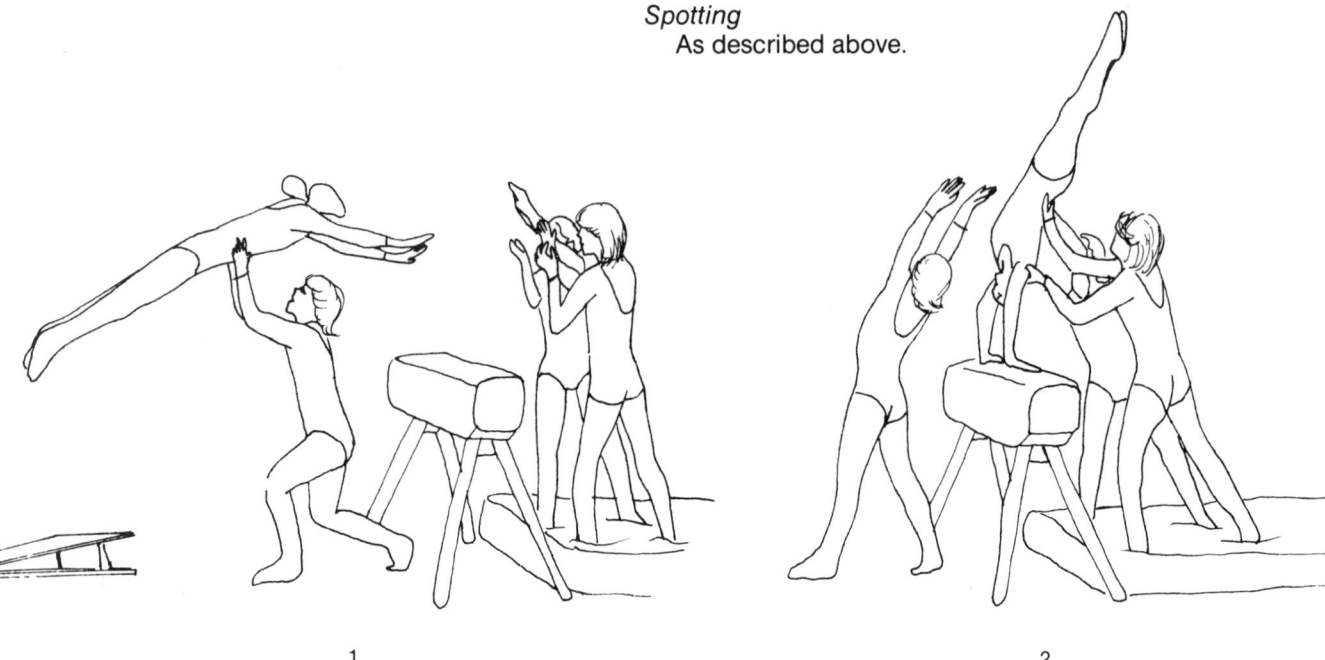

Handspring with three spotters

E. Rules and Basic Judging

The rules for Artistic Gymnastics are established by the International Federation of Gymnastics (F.I.G.). Very often the rules are modified to accommodate local needs. These changes are usually made to assist gymnasts and instructors who are at beginning levels. The following basic information is, however, based on current F.I.G. rules, and is presented for classroom information only. For a more detailed discussion, consult the F.I.G. *Code of Points for Women.*

1. Judges

Routines are evaluated by four judges, one of whom is a head judge. Each judge computes her score independently of the others and then gives her score to the head judge. If the head judge accepts all scores, the highest and lowest of the four scores is eliminated and the two middle scores are averaged for a final score. This is the only score known to the gymnast.

2. Compulsory and Optional Exercises

Compulsory exercises are those routines established by local organizations (regional, national or international) and performed by all gymnasts. A list of general faults and their penalties is also established. Gymnasts perform a compulsory vault, and compulsory routines in uneven bars, balance beam, and floor exercise. The floor exercise routine is performed to a compulsory music selection.

In addition to the compulsory exercises or routines, each gymnast must perform optional exercises. These include two optional vaults (the vaults may or may not be the same), and optional routines in the other three events.

F.I.G. designates skills as "medium" or "superior" according to their levels of difficulty, and the optional exercises should contain three skills at the superior level and four skills at the medium difficulty level. The optional exercises or routines are chosen by the gymnast, in consultation with her coach or coaches. The routines must not be the same as the compulsory ones, and must not use the same mount or dismount used in the compulsory exercises. The music for the floor routine is optional.

Both the compulsory and the optional routines are scored out of 10 points, using tenths of a point. The only exception to this is in the case of vaults. Each vault has been given a point value out of 10 based on its difficulty. The vaults in this case are scored out of the given value.

The levels of difficulty and the point value of the various vaults are reflected in the Code of Points. The breakdown is as follows:
Composition (What you do)

Value of Difficulty	3.00
3 superior at 0.6 = 1.8	
4 medium at 0.3 = 1.2	
3.0	
Originality and value of connection	1.50
Value of general composition of exercise	.50
	5.00
Execution (How you do it)	
Execution and Amplitude	4.00
General Impression	1.00
	5.00

General faults include poor positioning of the feet, legs, body, and arms, and the penalties are as follows:

Small	0.10 to 0.20 points
Medium	0.30 to 0.40 points
Serious	0.50 points

Other penalties for poor landings or for falling apply to all events and include the following:

Touching the floor with one or two hands	0.30
Fall on the knees or seat	0.50
Landing with hops or steps	0.10 - 0.20
Fall from the apparatus	0.50

3. Rules for Specific Events

a) Floor Exercise

The floor exercise must be original. The gymnast must utilize the 12 meter by 12 meter (approximately 12 yard by 12 yard) area without going outside of the boundaries. The length of the floor routine is one minute to one minute, thirty seconds. The choice of music is unlimited and should complement the type of movements performed and the gymnast's personality. Some basic penalties include the following:

Exercise too long	0.30
Exercise too short	0.05 per second
Repetition of a missed element	0.50
Fall	0.50

| SKILL | DESCRIPTION | TEACHING TECHNIQUES AND OBSERVATION POINTS |

b) Uneven Parallel Bars

Bar skills involve swinging and circling moves with releases and re-grasps, and the routine may include from ten to eighteen movements. There must be a balance of movement from one bar to the other. This event is not timed. Some basic penalties include the following:

Stops	0.20
Extra Swings	0.50
Releasing one hand without supplementary support	0.30
Releasing one hand with supplementary support	0.50

c) Balance Beam

The routine must show balance and body control, and must use the complete length of the beam. The gymnast must incorporate tumbling movements as well as dance movements. Variations in elevation and rhythm must be used.

Judges look for amplitude (height and extension) on jumps, leaps, and so on. A maximum of three stops is allowed. The duration is one minute, fifteen seconds to one minute, thirty-five seconds. Some basic penalties include the following:

Additional stops	0.20
Monotony of rhythm	0.20
Monotony for the duration	0.50
Unnecessary movements of trunk to maintain balance	0.30
Unnecessary movements of arms or legs to maintain balance	0.20
Poor head position	0.20

d) Vault

Each vault is assigned a point value by F.I.G. The gymnast performs two vaults, which may be the same or different. The judges evaluate both vaults and the best score is taken for the final mark.

Penalties are established for the different stages of the vault; run and take off, pre-flight, support on the horse, post-flight, landing. These are very detailed and specific. For basic vaults, most of the penalties will be given for general faults.

Chapter Four
Planning The Program

A. Organizing the Class

1. Use a Consistent Format
Set up the unit so that each lesson uses basically the same format. In this way the students become familiar with the procedure and time used for instructions is minimized. The following format is recommended:

- a) Equipment set up — as soon as students come into the gymnasium
- b) Attendance
- c) Warm-up, conditioning
- d) Mass tumbling — review
- e) New material — demonstrations and note-taking
- f) Culminating activity — students work on individual programs, instructor rotates or remains at one apparatus, depending on the requirements of the lesson.

2. Use of Stations
For the culminating activity, the instructor may wish to divide the class into groups that will move through different stations. Or the students may work very well moving freely on their own from one station to another.

The station approach works very well for large numbers. A variety of stations can be set up to accommodate as many participants as possible. For example, the following ten stations could easily accommodate a class of thirty-six students with three or four to a station. Each group could spend ten minutes at each station and cover all ten in two lessons.

1. Low vault without beat board
2. Beat board and landing pit (practice run and jump)
3. Uneven parallel bars
4. Parallel bar, one bar removed to become low bar
5. Tumbling mats
6. Benches (use for forward rolls, etc.)
7. Balance beam
8. Lines on floor for practicing routines or turns, etc.
9. Resource materials — an area for reading books, studying loop films or reviewing Personal Gymnastics Booklets (see Appendix II).
10. Conditioning area — an area for doing extra conditioning exercises. For example, a time clock can be provided to enable students to work on the Canada Fitness exercises.

3. Co-ed Classes
Although this handbook focuses on Women's Artistic Gymnastics, the following comments are included for the benefit of those teachers who are teaching co-ed gymnastics classes.

Teaching gymnastics to co-ed classes, especially at the junior high level, can present some unique problems. The junior high student tends to be very self-conscious, more concerned with appearance and "who is watching" than learning the basics of gymnastics. This situation makes it especially difficult to teach the dance portion of Women's Artistic Gymnastics because the girls will feel apprehensive of their male audience.

The demands on the instructor are much greater in a co-ed situation because there are six events for men and four events for women. It is difficult to be knowledgeable about all the apparatus, let alone to be able to teach all the events in a four- to six-week unit.

The following suggestions could enhance the teaching of co-ed gymnastics:

- a) Reduce the requirements for the course.
  - i) Reduce the number of skills on each piece of apparatus.
  - ii) Divide the gymnastics unit into two sections — tumbling and apparatus.
  - iii) Have the girls choose two out of four of the women's events and the boys, three out of six of the men's events.
- b) Have the unit run for two months and combine it with aerobics. While the girls are doing gymnastics, the boys could be running and vice versa.
- c) Do not emphasize dance skills to the same extent.
- d) Have girls spot girls and boys spot boys, or the seriousness of the situation may be lost.
- e) Team teach with a male colleague.

Teaching a co-ed gymnastics class presents a series of challenges to the physical educator which require careful planning and organization if a positive outcome is to result.

B. Lesson Plans

This section has been divided into two parts. The ten Lesson Plans in the first section have been developed to assist in the organization of a gymnastics unit. These lessons are meant to serve only as a suggestion; they are by no means the only method of presentation. In some instances a unit may include more or fewer lessons, and sometimes the instructor may wish to expand those lessons for which a particular group of students requires more time. The lessons have been developed for the Level I or Beginner level. The second section presents Lesson Plans designed to accommodate more than one level.

To provide one example of how to develop instructional lessons for this handbook, all lessons have been structured to utilize a teaching aid called a Personal Gymnastics Booklet. Individual instructors will elect to modify this approach as their own situation dictates. An example of a booklet for each of the levels has been included in Appendix II. Color coding the first page will facilitate identification of the appropriate booklet for a particular level.

Level One — white.
Level Two — blue.
Level Three — yellow.
Level Four — orange.

A detailed discussion of the use of this teaching aid can be found in Appendix II.

These Lesson Plans have been developed for the following situation:
a) Class size: 30-35
b) Length of lesson: 45-50 minutes. 10-15 minutes for dressing, setting apparatus up and attendance.
c) Facility and Apparatus: Space to accommodate tumbling mats, 1 balance beam, uneven bars, 1 Swedish box or vaulting horse, 1 beat board, 1 landing pad, individual mats.

Lesson One - Introduction

1. Introduction - 20 min.

For some students there will be a certain amount of apprehension about the gymnastics unit. It is therefore important that the instructor explains the requirements for the course, the class organization, and the methods of evaluation at the first meeting. The following topics should be discussed:
a) Why do gymnastics?
   i) Fun
   ii) Individualized, does not require a partner
   iii) Provides the opportunity to develop flexibility, strength, grace, balance, power, endurance
   iv) Provides an opportunity for students to assist each other in spotting or critically observing each other's skills
   v) Provides an opportunity for a unique body movement and spatial awareness
b) Personal Equipment
   i) Clothing should be loose, leotards are ideal
   ii) No slippery footwear
   iii) Hair must be tied back, no jewelery
c) Apparatus
   i) Women's gymnastics is divided into four events - Floor Exercise, Uneven Parallel Bars, Balance Beam, Vault. Floor Exercise includes Tumbling and Dance.
   ii) Brief description of apparatus, including mats and beat board
   iii) Use of magnesium chalk
d) Explanation of levels system and organization
   i) Issue and discuss Personal Gymnastics Booklets (see Appendix II)
   ii) Class should read the first page of the booklet
   iii) Explain basic requirements
e) Safety - Use of Apparatus and Spotting

The setting up of apparatus should be begun by students as soon as they enter the gymnasium for their lesson. It usually takes about 15 minutes. The class should put up all the apparatus and discuss where it is to be placed and where it is to be put away. The setting up may be done by designating certain students to look after a particular apparatus or on a random basis.

A discussion of the importance of spotting should be included here.

2. Objective

By the end of Lesson One, the students should be able to demonstrate the following:
a) Putting up, and putting away of all apparatus
b) A proper gymnastics warm-up
c) The basic gymnastics positions - tuck, straddle, pike and layout.

3. Warm-up - 15 min.

Discuss the components of every gymnastics warm-up — cardio-vascular exercises, flexibility and stretching, and strength exercises. Dance exercises and basic locomotor activities should be included in the cardio-vascular section of the warm-up.

To help encourage students to attend to the exercises, the instructor may initially lead the warm-up in a follow-the-leader approach for the first week of the unit. From then on the instructor should designate one of the students to lead the warm-up (see pages 16-17 and the Sample Warm-Up in Appendix III).

During this first lesson the instructor should discuss the importance of static stretching as opposed to ballistic stretching and the process of stretching every joint in the body. An indication of the number of repetitions for the strength exercises should also be made at this time.

The basic gymnastics positions are also introduced during this time.

4. Review

This section is omitted for Lesson One.

5. New Material

For Lesson One the setting up of equipment and warm-up would be considered the new material.

6. Culmination - 5 min.

Apparatus away
Collection of Personal Gymnastics Booklets
Outline Lesson Two

Lesson Two - Tumbling and Floor Exercise

1. Introduction

Lesson Two will introduce the event which is basic to all other events - tumbling and floor exercise. For this lesson, the students need only put out the mats. It is best to introduce this equipment first, because it can accommodate the greatest number of students and does not involve the special safety precautions required for other apparatus.

If large wrestling mats are available, arrange them to form a large tumbling area.

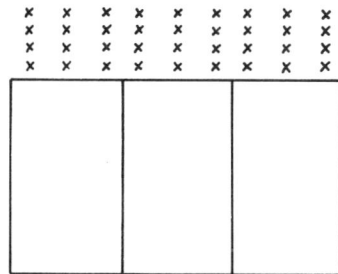

If wrestling mats are not available, arrange smaller mats width-ways in pairs and have 6-8 students work across each pair.

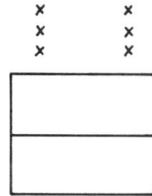

2. Objectives

By the end of Lesson Two the students will:
a) Demonstrate the ability to do the warm-up skills.
b) Have an understanding of the basic requirements for tumbling and floor exercise - forward roll, backward roll, headstand, handstand with spotting.
c) Demonstrate the ability to spot each other for the basic tumbling requirements and understand the safety precautions to be taken when using tumbling equipment.

3. Warm-up - 10 min.

Regular gymnastics warm-up led by the instructor. Include the basic locomotor movements: walking, running, hopping, skipping, jumping, leaping, galloping, sliding.

4. Review - 5 min.

Basic body positions (tuck, straddle, pike, layout)
Basic components to warm-up.

5. New Material - 30 min.

a) Class will sit down with pencils and Personal Gymnastics Booklets to take notes on demonstration and spotting of the basic tumbling requirements.
b) Students work on the skills, spotting and correcting each other, as instructor corrects class as a whole. Students should attempt skills only as the instructor requests, and should not proceed ahead of the class.

6. Culmination - 5 min.

Mats away
Collection of Personal Gymnastics Booklets
Closing remarks: the next session will be the uneven parallel bars.

Lesson Three: Uneven Parallel Bars

1. Introduction

The uneven parallel bars are seldom seen in the elementary schools, so many students are anxious to learn what can be done with them. For this reason it is best to introduce them immediately after the tumbling. The beam, uneven bars and tumbling area are required for this lesson.

2. Objectives

By the end of Lesson Three the students will:
a) Demonstrate an understanding of the skills introduced in Lesson Two.
b) Have the opportunity to demonstrate the basic tumbling requirements in a testing situation.
c) Understand the basic requirements for the uneven bars and the necessary safety precautions.
d) Demonstrate the ability to spot each other for the basic uneven bar skills.

3. Warm-up - 8 min.

Regular gymnastics warm-up.

4. Review - 2 min.

Mass tumbling - review basic requirements for tumbling.

5. New Material - 30 min.

a) As part of the mass tumbling, introduce a variety of skills from the Additional Skills list in the Personal Gymnastics Booklets (see Appendix II).
forward roll, half turn backward roll, half turn forward roll, backward roll to knee scale.
Class should practice these skills for 5 minutes.

b) Class should sit down around uneven bars with pencils and Personal Gymnastics Booklets and take notes on the demonstration of the basic skills on the uneven bars, spotting techniques, and safety requirements. The demonstration is best done by a student while the instructor spots and verbally instructs. This demonstration will take about 15 minutes.
c) Divide class in half - send half to tumbling area to practice tumbling, and test each other, and divide the remaining half into two lines. Have one student from each line attempt the basic skills, spotted if necessary by the person next in line. The instructor should correct verbally where necessary. By putting two students on the bar at the same time the lines are kept moving and each student should manage more than one attempt within the 10 minutes allowed for this stage.
d) Rotate the tumbling group to the bars.

6. Culmination - 10 min.

Free time - divide the class into three groups, send one to the tumbling area, one to the bars, and one to the beam to explore this new apparatus. Rotate groups after two minutes.
Apparatus away.
Collect Personal Gymnastics Booklets.

Lesson Four: Balance Beam

1. Introduction

By using modified apparatus such as benches, an instructor can easily accommodate any sized class for the introduction of the balance beam. Instructors should also stress the progression from the floor, to the bench, and finally to a regulation beam set at a height of approximately one meter (3'). This allows the student to master the skill safely and confidently before attempting it at a height.

2. Objectives

By the end of Lesson Four the students will:
a) Understand the basic requirements and safety precautions for the balance beam.
b) Demonstrate the ability to spot each other for the basic requirements on the balance beam.
c) Be provided with the opportunity to be tested on those skills they feel they have mastered.

3. Warm-up - 7 min.

Regular gymnastics warm-up, led by the instructor. At this time choose a student to lead the warm-up in the next class. Briefly review components of a good warm-up.

4. Review - 3 min.

Mass tumbling - review basic requirements for tumbling and skills introduced in the previous lesson from the Additional Skills list (Appendix II).

5. New Material - 35 min.

a) Set out the balance beam apparatus so that after the students have travelled along one bench (or beam) they can move directly to the next one (see diagram).

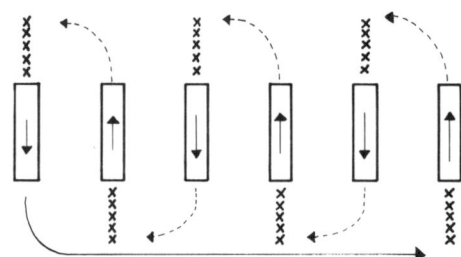

For example, the instructor demonstrates or discusses the forward walk, the groups move along the apparatus, and then stop at the next piece of apparatus to wait for instructions on the next skill.
b) Seat the class around the apparatus with pencils and their Personal Gymnastics Booklets to take notes on the specific techniques of the skills, the safety precautions, and the spotting before they attempt the skills.
c) Each student will attempt to do the skills using the formation outlined in a) above.
d) Before introducing the forward roll on the balance beam, move the class back to the mats for the instructions. A chalk mark on the mats can be used to determine if the gymnast is rolling straight as is required on the beam. The chalk from the mat will be transferred to the gymnast's back and it should be straight.

6. Culmination

This is a long lesson but should any time remain, allow gymnasts to move freely to the apparatus of their choice. For those who wish to be tested on a particular skill, it may be done at this time.
Apparatus away. Collect Personal Gymnastics Booklets.
Closing remarks: The next lesson will cover the final event, the vault.

Lesson Five: Vault

1. Introduction

Because many girls are nervous about vaulting, it is important to emphasize that no one will be asked to perform any skill that they are not physically or psychologically able to handle. Point out that performer safety is the prime consideration. This will be the first time most girls have seen a beat board, so spend some time introducing them to approaching and rebounding from the beat board. Do not use the horse at this stage.
When the Swedish box is introduced, remove the bottom level (or levels) for the initial instruction. As the performers gain confidence, the levels can be added until the box reaches regulation height.

2. Objectives

By the end of Lesson Five the students will:
a) Understand the basic requirements and safety precautions for the vault.
b) Demonstrate the ability to spot each other for the squat vault.
c) Have been tested on a minimum of one tumbling skill and one skill on each of the bars, and the balance beam.

3. Warm-up - 7 min.

Regular gymnastics warm-up, led by a student. Instructor should correct the technique and watch that all areas are covered.

4. Review - 5 min.

Mass Tumbling
Review the forward roll on the balance beam and the spotting technique. Use the tumbling area.

5. New Material - 35 min.

a) Seat class on the floor around the vaulting station, taking notes on basic requirements, spotting techniques, and safety procedures.
b) After the discussion and a demonstration of the basic requirements, divide the class into four groups. Send one group to each piece of apparatus for about 5 minutes. The instructor will stay at the vaulting station and go over the skills with each girl as she rotates with her group to the vault.

From the very start, each gymnast should get into the habit of remaining at the vault and spotting for the next girl. This way the instructor can observe both her vaulting and her spotting techniques and make the necessary corrections.

Be alert for any student whose fear of the vault may cause her to injure herself. Please refer to Section D - Modified Programs, for further details.

c) Be specific about what the students are to do at each piece of apparatus. Insist that they work only on the static positions:
  tumbling — headstand, basic body positions, handstand with spotting
  bars — front support mount, long hang
  beam — lunge, knee scale
This is also a good opportunity for testing to take place.

6. Culmination - 3 min.

Closing Remarks: We have now covered all four pieces of apparatus. The remainder of the lessons will be spent on individual instruction and testing. Remind students about the written test to be given in Lesson Seven. Students must know the names of the skills and should spend some time going over their notes on spotting techniques and safety.
Apparatus away.

Lesson Six: "Trouble Clinics" — Skill Testing

1. Introduction

All four events have now been introduced. The remainder of the unit can now be spent on assisting those students who are having difficulties, perfecting the basic requirements in each event, skill testing, and introducing additional skills.

2. Objectives

By the end of Lesson Six the students will:
a) Have received individual instruction in the areas in which they are experiencing difficulty
b) Have the opportunity to be tested in those areas in which they are prepared.

3. Warm-up - 10 min.

Regular gymnastics warm-up led by a student.

4. Review - 5 min.

Mass Tumbling. For example:
a) forward roll, half turn, backward roll
b) forward roll, full turn, forward roll
c) free forward roll
d) forward straddle roll
e) forward roll, headstand, forward roll
f) back roll to knee scale
g) forward roll to splits.

5. New Material - 25 min.

a) Problem Sheet
Explain that you would like spend time working with those students who have difficulty in one area or another — you might like to say you will offer "clinics" at each piece of apparatus. Start at the tumbling area with all those students who would like additional instruction in that event. Then proceed to the uneven bars, to the beam, and finally to the vault. Those students not having difficulty can move more freely to their choice of the apparatus not in use and work on perfecting their skills and testing each other.

6. Culmination - 5 min.

Have the students sit down with their booklets and look over the notes for the written test next class. Explain that the test will include :
a) the names of the skills
b) spotting techniques
c) safety rules and regulations

Be available to answer questions about any of the above.
Apparatus away.

Lesson Seven: Written Test

1. Introduction

Most of this class will be taken up by the written test, and for this reason the order of activity has been changed. Please see Chapter Five, Section B for a more detailed explanation of the test.

2. Objectives

By the end of Lesson Seven the students will have:
a) Written a test.
b) Demonstrated their ability to do their own total body warm-up.

3. New Material - 25 min.

Administer written test.

4. Warm-up - 10 min.

Have each student conduct her own total body warm-up. Students have had the opportunity to see several proper warm-ups and should now be able to do a good general warm-up on their own.

5. Review - 5 min.
Mass tumbling.

6. Culmination - 10 min.

Provide a film on Gymnastics or a video tape of a Gymnastics meet.

Lesson Eight: Additional Skills on Apparatus — Skill Testing

1. Introduction

The introduction of additional skills on the apparatus will be determined by how quickly your students have picked up the basic skills for Level I. If the majority need additional instruction in the basics, use this lesson in this manner.

However, more advanced students may be interested in the additional skills listed in their booklets. The introduction of these additional skills could be an optional part of the lesson, allowing some students an opportunity to work individually.

Reserve a portion of the lesson for testing students on the basics. This lesson provides the opportunity to check closely the performance level of the skills.

2. Objectives

By the end of Lesson Eight the students will:
a) Have observed and understood many of the additional skills on the uneven bars, balance beam, and vault.
b) Have had the opportunity to be tested on the basic requirements.

3. Warm-up - 5 min.
Regular warm-up.

4. Review - 5 min.

Mass tumbling. During the mass tumbling any of the additional skills in tumbling that have not been covered can be introduced.

5. New Material

a) Uneven parallel bars - 10 min.
   Choose a variety of the additional skills from Level I and present them to class. The spotting of these skills must be presented as well.
   Example:
   i) skin the cat
   ii) pullover mount to front support
   iii) single knee drop to hock swing
   iv) from front support to stride support
   At this time, a combination of several of the elements could be suggested.
   Example:
   i) pullover mount, to stride support, to single knee drop, skin the cat.
   ii) pullover mount, cast rearwards to stand
b) Balance beam — 10 min.
   i) V-sit with support of hands
   ii) tuck jump dismount
   Examples of combinations:
   i) front support mount, V-sit, stand, four steps walking on toes, lunge, tuck dismount
   ii) front support mount, knee scale, stand half turn, two steps backward, half turn, two-foot jump, straight jump dismount
c) Vault — 10 min.
   When introducing additional skills on the vault, encourage students to work at the regulation height of 110 cm. (3'6") if they are not already doing so. They should practice long, hard run-ups and work at moving the beat board away from the horse.

6. Culmination - 10 min.

Spend the remainder of the class time testing. Students who wish to be tested hand their booklets to the instructor open to the event that they wish to be tested on. The instructor works through the stack of booklets in the order in which they were received. Apparatus away.

Lesson Nine: Dance and Skill Testing

1. Introduction

By this time in the unit, the students should be more confident about performing in front of their peers and perhaps a little more receptive to learning some dance techniques.

Present the dance on the bare floor. If your apparatus must be left up, push it to one side.

Spend the remainder of the class time on skill testing.

2. Objective

By the end of Lesson Nine the students will:
a) Have an understanding of correct body posture and dance technique for floor exercises.
b) Perform within their capability a variety of dance elements appropriate to Level I floor exercise skills.
c) Have had an opportunity to be tested on basic requirements.
d) Have worked on additional skills learned in the previous lesson.

3. Warm-up – 10 min.

A general gymnastics warm-up led by the instructor using a follow-the-leader approach. The cardio-vascular section of the warm-up should include the basic locomotor skills, stressing correct posture, body alignment and arm positions throughout. This can be done in a circle formation with the instructor moving inside the circle in the opposite direction. This enables you to see each one of the girls and provide corrections. Music, even just background music, would enhance this lesson on dance.

Example:
   i) walk, arms loosely swinging at sides
   ii) run — long steps, short steps, four long, four short
   iii) walk on toes, arms above head
   iv) walk knees bent, head down
   v) skip forward
   vi) skip backwards (half turn first)
   vii) walk two steps, half turn (repeat), arms above head on turn
   viii) gallop, two times right, two times left
   ix) walk (to catch breath), arms in 'V' above head
   x) sliding, slide two times, half turn (repeat)

4. Review

Regular stretching.

5. New Material - 15 min.

a) Introduce the basic ballet positions. Explain that the arm positions are all curved when used with the ballet positions, but can be straight when used in floor routines to provide a variety of positions, either horizontal, vertical or lateral.

Note: At this point your students may become self-conscious and silly. Try to be understanding of their feelings of awkwardness, but firm about the need for cooperation when you are introducing the material.

b) To practice the skills, line up in pairs across the width of the gymnasium (see diagram).

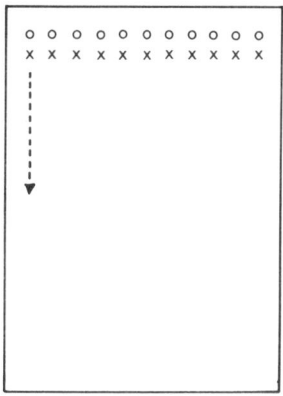

Demonstrate and explain each skill. The X's move as a group down the length of the gym, performing the skill. When they are halfway down, the O's proceed. The skill is repeated the entire length of the gym.
   i) high kick (arms up), lunge (arms come forward to describe a circle), three long running steps (arms optional)
   ii) gallop right, gallop left, gallop right, full turn left (arms optional)
   iii) skip forward four steps, half turn, skip backwards four steps
   iv) run, run, leap (opposite arm forward to leg)
   v) waltz step

6. Culmination – 20 min.

Skill testing

Lesson Ten: Free Time and Skill Testing

1. Introduction

Prior to this final lesson, the instructor should take time to look over the Personal Gymnastics Booklets. Remind students who are behind in skill testing that they must complete their tests during this class. Those students who have been on a modified program should also be checked.

The final lesson of the unit should be as unstructured as possible. Those who have finished with their skill testing may be free to try additional skills on the apparatus of their choice. Another suggestion would be to have them look over the Level II requirements and perhaps attempt some of these.

The teaching program itself may also be evaluated.

2. **Objective**

    By the end of Lesson Ten, the students will:
    a) Have had an opportunity to work freely on the event(s) of their choice.
    b) Finished any skill testing to be done.
    c) Examined the Level II program.

3. **Warm-up – 10 min.**

    Individual warm-up

4. **Review**

    Omitted to allow as much free time as possible.

5. **New Material**

    Omitted to allow as much free time as possible.

6. **Culmination – 35 min.**

    Free time and skill testing
    Closing remarks: Finish the class with a five-minute open discussion of the Level I unit. Discuss the unit with a particular reference to the positive aspects of each class and their particular strengths. Ask for input, either verbal or written. Discuss Level II.
    Apparatus away.

C. Multi-Leveled Classes

A class that includes students of varying abilities and several skill levels requires more organization and preparation on the part of the instructor. However, it also means the instructor has available students from Levels II and III to demonstrate skills, to help with spotting, and to assist in testing. Gymnasts who are familiar with the apparatus and the basic procedures of a gymnastics unit can assist lower-level gymnasts, and this in itself will be a time saver for the instructor.

Young gymnasts are quickly bored by repetition of skills that they have learned in a lower level. Although some review work is necessary, it should be brief. Students must be given the opportunity to learn new and more difficult skills appropriate to their level.

In a multi-level class, the basic lessons can be modified in the following ways:

1. Warm-up

    Usually students warm-up together regardless of level. However, if you wish to give the Level IV gymnasts a little extra freedom, you might consider allowing them to warm-up on their own every once in a while. This will give them the opportunity to demonstrate their knowledge of the principles of a proper warm-up.

    Explain the basic principles and exercises in the first lesson, and then select a gymnast from the highest level to lead the warm-up in succeeding classes. Gradually work through the class until you reach the Level I gymnasts.

2. Mass Tumbling

    During this part of the lesson, have the class line up according to their levels so that all Level I's are together, Level II's, and so on. This makes it easier to evaluate and correct their performance.

    At the beginning of the mass tumbling, all levels may do the same skills, but then the instructor should provide more difficult skills appropriate for each level.

3. Introducing new skills

    Try to introduce the skills of all levels on a *single piece of apparatus* during one lesson. Initially all students should be present with their booklets to take notes on apparatus safety. After the Level I skills have been introduced, the Level I gymnasts should be sent to work on another piece of apparatus. After the Level II skills have been introduced, the Level II gymnasts should be sent to another piece of apparatus, and so on, until all levels have had their basic requirements introduced. This way each level reviews the skills of the level below and the correct criteria for testing.

    In grouping students for rotation at stations, try to assign equal numbers of performers to each piece of apparatus. Very often, the majority of gymnasts are Levels I and II, and there are very few at Levels III and IV.

4. Overall organization of the unit

    The increased number of skills that must be demonstrated and discussed limit the time available for individual attention. During the first five lessons, when skills are being introduced, the instructor will have to move quickly to cover all levels.

5. Sample lesson plan

Lesson Four: Balance Beam

If your class includes students at four different levels, the level plan for Lesson Four (see page 92) could be modified in the following ways:

1. **Introduction**

    See page 92.

2. **Objectives**

    See page 92.

3. **Warm-up - 7 min.**

    Regular gymnastics warm-up, led by Level III or IV gymnast. Select student to lead warm-up next day.

4. **Review mass tumbling – 3 min.**

    Have gymnasts lined up according to ability. A suggested mass tumbling sequence is outlined below:

    a) All — forward roll, half turn, forward roll
    b) All — forward straddle roll, half turn, backward straddle roll
    c) I and II — forward roll, full turn, forward roll
    d) III and IV — forward roll, full turn, cartwheel, quarter turn

d) I and II — Backward roll, half turn, headstand, forward roll
   III and IV — Straight leg backward roll, half turn, handstand, forward roll
e) I and II — Forward straddle roll, handstand
   III and IV — Round-off

5. New Material - 35 min.

See layout of equipment on page 62. All gymnasts sit down around beam with booklets and pencil.
  i) Discuss safety for all gymnasts. Gymnasts take notes.
  ii) Demonstrate and discuss basic requirements for Level I. Level I gymnasts take notes. Send Level I gymnasts to tumbling area to work on basic requirements.
  iii) Demonstrate and discuss basic requirements for Level II. Then send Level II's to tumbling area, and Level I's or to the uneven bars.
  iv) Demonstrate and discuss basic requirements for Levels III and IV. (Can be done together, because this will be a small group.) Go over the basic routine and explain additional routine requirements to the Level IV's. Leave the Level III's at the beam area and move the Level IV's to the vault for review.

6. Culmination

Depending on the amount of time available, you may wish to rotate groups or allow them to rotate freely to the apparatus of their choice. Encourage all gymnasts to be tested on the skills they have mastered.
Closing remarks — see page 92.

D. Modified Programs

In every gymnastics class there will be those girls who are very much afraid of gymnastics. Whether or not this fear seems justified, it is very real. Some reasons for fearing or disliking gymnastics may be:
  a) An unpleasant experience with gymnastics in the past
  b) An inability to control body weight
  c) An obvious lack of strength
  d) Shyness at performing in front of others.

The instructor must be quick to alleviate these fears if the gymnastics unit is to be a positive experience for these girls. The girl who is afraid is a hazard in the gymnastics class because she may change her mind in the middle of the skill and cause injury to herself or others.

The overweight girl poses a particularly difficult problem. Her attempts to perform some skills may embarrass her or her classmates, and it is often almost impossible for others to spot her.

A modified program adapted to an individual's capabilities is an invaluable aid. Sit down with the student in question and go over each of the skills. Determine which ones she finds difficult. Based on her answers and your own judgment of the situation, skills can be deleted or modified.

For example, a modified balance beam program might require that the skills be performed on the bench rather than the raised balance beam. In other words, the student may be required to perform only the lead-up to the skill. Or suggest that all skills will be tested with a spotter.

With much of the fear removed, the possibility of achieving success becomes much greater, and the student feels encouraged.

Students who have limited motor skill but regular attendance, knowledge and visible effort, may attain a passing grade, but explain that they must continue working at Level I until they have sufficient background to proceed to the next level.

Chapter Five
Evaluation

A. Introduction

Gymnastics is taught in circumstances that vary greatly from school to school depending on the facilities, the abilities of the students, and the expertise of the instructor. Because every class is in essence a multi-level class the consideration of individual differences is extremely important, not only in organizing lessons, but also in evaluating student progress. Development of an individualized evaluation system is therefore recommended.

Evaluation is the process of making judgments about the results of measurement in terms of the goals and objectives of a course, and it is a major responsibility of the physical education instructor. This chapter deals with the two main aspects of evaluation:

A. Individual Evaluation, including grading and reporting

B. Program Evaluation

B. Individual Evaluation

A gymnastics student must be evaluated at the start of the unit to determine at which level she will begin. It is recommended that all participants begin at Level I. However, for those who have some background in gymnastics the instructor may wish to have the student demonstrate an ability to perform the basic skills at various levels before deciding on placement. If a student is very talented, she will quickly progress through the levels until she is met with a challenge. At the same time, the instructor must also be aware of students who are finding Level I too difficult and for whom a modified Level I program will have to be designed.

Physical Education objectives are classified within the psychomotor, cognitive, and affective domains. Progress should be assessed during the program, as well as at the conclusion, to determine the extent to which these goals have been achieved. The instructor must determine the skills the students have developed, the knowledge they have acquired, and the values and the attitudes they have formed and expressed through their behavior. These are then evaluated in relation to the goals that have been set down by the instructor.

1. Psychomotor:

   To evaluate psychomotor skill progress, the instructor might consider the following:

   a) Is the skill performed with or without spotting?
   b) Is there one spotter or two?
   c) How well is the skill executed? ('Execution' means form. Are the legs straight? Toes pointed?)
   d) Is the skill performed with amplitude? ('amplitude' means height. Is the leap high? Is there height on the tuck jump on the beam?)
   e) Is there creativity in the placement of the arms? Head?
   f) Is there good balance and weight transfer?
   g) Is the skill performed smoothly? Lightly?
   h) Is there control in the landing?

2. Cognitive:

   Whether or not a written test is used in a gymnastics unit is a matter to be left entirely up to the instructor. As in other subject areas, the information from tests can be used to help determine whether or not the objectives of the course are being achieved. Are the participants learning the names of the skills? Are the participants familiar with specific spotting techniques? A written test can be very helpful in answering these questions.

   The test need not be a long one, and having the participants correct each other's test saves the instructor doing the marking.

   Two different types of tests are presented here. The first example (A) stresses the names of the skills and spotting techniques. The format is such that the instructor may use different skills for each class, thus providing variety. This type of test should be administered in the following manner:

   1. Fill out a blank test, choosing the skills that will be tested in any one particular class. Choose skills from all four apparatus.
   2. Select a member of the class who is able to perform each of the chosen skills. She will be your demonstrator. (Where the instructor is able to perform all the skills, a demonstrator is not necessary.)
   3. Have the students sit on the gymnasium floor, each with a blank copy of the test.
   4. Have the demonstrator perform the skill. The rest of the class watches and then writes the name of the skill and the spotting (if required) on their test papers.
   5. After the demonstrator has performed the skill she would write down the spotting description on her paper. (If the demonstrator performs the correct skill, this is her test of knowledge.)

In the second example (B), the questions are answered as for any other written test.

Items for Levels III and IV might include questions on judging and regulations for gymnasts, laid down by F.I.G. (International Gymnastics Federation).

A. GYMNASTICS KNOWLEDGE TEST

NAME: _____

1. Name of Skill _____
   Spotting _____
2. Name of Skill _____
   Spotting _____
3. Name of Skill _____
4. Name of Skill _____
5. Describe the spotting of the forward roll on the beam.
   _____
   _____
   _____
   _____
6. List four safety rules.
   (a) _____
   (b) _____
   (c) _____
   (d) _____

B. LEVEL II GYMNASTICS TEST

NAME: _____

1. List five safety rules for the gymnastics class.

5
   (a) _____
   (b) _____
   (c) _____
   (d) _____
   (e) _____

2. Describe the spotting technique for the pullover mount to front support on the uneven bars.

3
   _____
   _____
   _____

3. What is the lead-up skill to the straddle vault?

1
   _____

2
4. List two dance movements taught in Level II.
   (a) _____
   (b) _____
5. Name the dismount off the balance beam taught in Level II.
   _____

3
6. Describe the spotting techniques for the cartwheel.
   _____
   _____

TOTAL _____

3. Affective:

   In assessing attitudes, consider the following questions:
   a) What is the participant's attitude toward the putting up and the taking down of equipment.?
   b) What is the participant's attitude toward spotting?
   c) Does the participant take part willingly in all sessions?
   d) What is the participant's attitude toward learning new skills?
   e) Does the participant enjoy gymnastic activity?

Instructors are also required to assign grades to students. When selecting a grading system, the instructor must endeavor to provide the students with a process that is positive rather than negative, challenging rather than discouraging, and simple to administer and tabulate. A Personal Gymnastics Booklet (see Appendix II) is one method of meeting these requirements. It has several advantages.

a) The objectives and requirements of the courses are written up in the booklet as a reminder for each student.
b) The skills for testing, called Basic Requirements, are set out in the booklet. Usually, four to six skills are given for each piece of apparatus, but the list can easily be lengthened or shortened to suit the length of the gymnastics unit and the particular expertise of the instructor.

Not all of the skills listed in the Personal Gymnastics Booklets are described in this handbook. Many of the skills listed in the Additional Skills lists may be lead-ups or modified skills. For information on skills not described in the handbook, please refer to the reference material listed in Appendix I.

c) Using the booklets, students can test each other, and testing can start as soon as the unit begins. Those in higher levels can test those in the lower levels, with the instructor making spot checks. This avoids the problem of spending too much instruction time on skill testing, removes the pressure to check everyone at the end of the unit, and motivates the students to get all skills checked off.

d) The booklet system enables the instructor to justify all grades with documentation, thus making the assigning of grades more objective.
e) At any time throughout the gymnastics unit, the instructor can quickly go through the booklets to determine how the class is progressing. The instructor can readily see which skills are causing difficulties and which individuals are having problems. This facilitates adjustments in the instructional time to accommodate these needs. Check all booklets when the course reaches the halfway point to make sure the students are not leaving too much skill testing until the end.

The disadvantage, of course, is that skill testing can become very time consuming if students are permitted to request individual tests at any time. The instructor should establish clear guidelines — testing of a particular skill will take place only at one time, and anyone who obviously needs more work on a skill may not request a follow-up test until the recommended practice has been completed.

C. Program Evaluation

When the gymnastics program as a whole is evaluated, the following questions should be considered:
1. How have the participants progressed?
2. Were the skills presented in the most logical manner?
3. Were the needs of a variety of learners met?
4. Was there flexibility in providing instruction to the class as a whole, in small groups, and with individuals?
5. Was the method of record keeping effective?
6. Were the setting and conditions of the gymnastics program suitable? Safe?
7. How did the gymnastics program contribute to the school and district program?
8. What impact did it have on the community?

Appendix I
Reference Material

A. Books

Canadian Gymnastics Federation Development Program.

Book I Participation (Red-White-Blue Levels).

Book II (Men's) Achievement (Merit-Bronze-Silver-Gold Levels).

Book III (Women's) Achievement (Merit-Bronze-Silver-Gold Levels).

Coaching Certification Manual, Level II. T. Kinsman (ed.), CGF, 1978.

Carr, Gerald A. *Safety in Gymnastics. A manual of safety and spotting techniques for elementary and intermediate gymnastics.* North Vancouver: Hancock House Publishers, 1980.

Cooper, Phyllis. *Feminine Gymnastics*. 2nd Edition. Minnesota: Burgess Publishing Company, 1973.

Hartley, Sandra. *Training, Conditioning, Flexibility Work for Women's Competitive Gymnastics.* Vanier City, Ontario: Coaching Association of Canada, N.d.

Ryan, Dr. Frank. *Gymnastics for Girls*. Penguin Books and Viking Press, U.S.A., 1977

Schmid, Andrea Bodo and Blanche Jessen Drury. *Gymnastics for Women.* 4th Edition. Palo Alto: Mayfield Publishing Company, 1977.

Taylor, Bryce, B. Bajin and T. Zivic. *Olympic Gymnastics for Men and Women.* Englewood Cliffs, N.J.: Prentice-Hall, 1971.

B. Films

8 mm., 16 mm., and strip films on Olympic championships, routines and individual skills and progressions are available from the following sources:

The Athletic Institute, 705 Merchandise Mart, Chicago, Illinois 60654.

Frank Endo, 12200 S. Berendo Avenue, Los Angeles, California 90044.

C. Journals

International Gymnast, Sundby Sports Publications, P.O. Box 110, Santa Monica, California.

Contains teaching techniques and coaching points. The photographs are excellent for use on bulletin boards.

D. Wall Charts

Charts which offer diagrams of skills and teaching techniques can be obtained from the following sources:

AMF American Athletic Equipment Division, 2000 American Avenue, Jefferson, Iowa 50129.

Nisse Corporation, 930 - 27th Avenue, S.W. Cedar Rapids, Iowa 52406.

W.M. Productions, P.O. Box 10573, Denver Colorado 80210.

The United States Gymnastics Safety Association, 17241 Dulles International Airport, Washington, D.C., 20041.

E. Gymnastics Associations

The following associations provide up to date information regarding the National Coaching Certification Program. This program provides courses throughout the province, for the certification of gymnastics coaches.

a) British Columbia Gymnastics Association (BCGA)
   1200 Hornby Street, Vancouver, B.C.

b) Canadian Gymnastic Federation (CGF)
   333 River Road, Vanier, Ontario K1L 8B9

Appendix II
Personal Gymnastics Booklet

Booklets, charts, and lists of skills are all used in teaching gymnastics. After experimenting with various methods, the author has found the Personal Gymnastics Booklet to be a valuable teaching aid. The following description and the sample booklet are intended to introduce this method of teaching. A different booklet is provided for each level of gymnastics from I to IV.

Each boolet lists the skills for that level on each piece of apparatus. The skills are presented in two lists, basic requirements and additional skills. The basic requirements are those skills that should be mastered by the gymnast and tested before moving on to the next level. The basic requirements found in the Personal Gymnastics Booklet are only suggestions and the list may be changed to accommodate the instructor's expertise and time restraints.

The list of Additional Skills is provided for those gymnasts who are able to complete the basic requirements in a short time and require additional material appropriate to that level to work on. Some of the additional skills are variations of the basic requirements, while others are lead-ups to the basic requirements of the next level. Details of those additional skills that are not described in the handbook can be found in the reference books listed in Appendix 1.

Space is available for the tester to initial the skill when it has been mastered by the participant.

Space has also been provided for students to take notes about each piece of apparatus, and about the safety rules as the skills are introduced. This provides the instructor with written evidence that safety and correct spotting techniques were covered and stressed throughout the unit. Although it cannot be shown here, each event should have a separate page in the booklet so that there is plenty of room to take notes.

The front page of the booklet describes the basic philosophy and requirements of the course. Use the same front page for each level by simply circling the appropriate level in the heading GYMNASTICS I II III IV.

The system has advantages and disadvantages, some of which are listed here:

Advantages:
1. Each booklet is personal and geared to the participant's particular level of ability. The material to be covered is clearly laid out for the student.
2. A record of skills mastered by participants is available to the instructor and the participant. This is helpful in determining:
    a) how quickly the participant or group as a whole is progressing,
    b) which areas require additional instruction,
    c) an appropriate grade for the end of the unit.
3. A record of spotting skills, teaching techniques and safety practices is available for the student throughout the unit.
4. The booklet makes it easier to accommodate various levels within the same group because each program is clearly laid out and participants can work on their own, and at their own speed.

Disadvantages:
1. Involves time for evaluation.
2. Booklets must be collected after every class.
3. Involves time for duplicating and collating booklets at the beginning of the unit.

Some of the disadvantages can be overcome by using the following suggestions:
1. Have one person responsible for collecting all booklets at the end of the class. This eliminates the problem of missing or lost booklets.
2. Begin testing in the first week. There will be many students ready to show they can already perform several of the skills. Additional information regarding testing procedures can be found in Chapter Five —Evaluation.
3. When duplicating booklets, run off enough for two years at a time. Always run off more Level I and II booklets than III and IV.

The booklets might be organized as follows:

Name _____

Block _____

GYMNASTICS I, II, III, IV

Gymnastics, more than any other activity, requires maximum effort from each participant. It is impossible for the teacher to stand over you throughout the entire period putting you through the skills. There isn't any reason for anyone to be sitting around on the floor unless you have mastered each and every skill listed. If this is the case, see me and I will provide additional skills for you to work on.

The building and performing of routines on the apparatus is a difficult task. Therefore, in Gymnastics I & II the emphasis is placed on learning the skills, not on building routines. You will be required to learn the names of the skills and a short written test will be given. A passing grade will not be given unless the basic requirements are learned. Students in a higher level may evaluate students in lower levels.

In Gymnastics I & II the evaluation will be as follows:
1. Must learn and be evaluated on all basic requirements on all apparatus.
2. Write a written test.

In Gymnastics III I have provided you with routines for each apparatus which must be learned. There is a check list as well. A written test will be given.

In Gymnastics IV you will be required to make a routine for each apparatus as well as learn the skills in your check list. You may choose to use the Level III routines to get you started and make changes according to your ability. A written test will be given.

Your mark in the course will be dependent on the following:
1. Attitude — effort, cooperation, etc.
2. Improvement — if you have made any advancement in your ability to perform skills.
3. Knowledge Test — there will be a short test on the names of the skills and spotting techniques.
4. Skill — based on the requirements for your course.

Note: At this point I would like to stress the importance of execution as well as difficulty. By execution we mean "how well" the skill is performed i.e., straight legs and pointed toes.

Difficulty and execution will be given "equal consideration."

BOOKLET I

Floor Exercise — Level I

A. BASIC REQUIREMENTS
- ☐☐ 1. Basic body positions: (tuck, pike, straddle, layout)
- ☐☐ 2. Forward roll — tuck
- ☐☐ 3. Backward roll to stand — backward roll — tuck
- ☐☐ 4. Headstand
- ☐☐ 5. Handstand (with spotting)

B. ADDITIONAL SKILLS

Tumbling:
- ☐☐ a) Back bend (push up from lying)
- ☐☐ b) Splits front (right and left) and side
- ☐☐ c) Roll back and forth in tuck position
- ☐☐ d) Above skill and straighten legs, touch toes on floor above head, hands under shoulders
- ☐☐ e) Forward roll (extend legs after push)
- ☐☐ f) Forward roll with jump — forward roll
- ☐☐ g) Forward roll to half turn
- ☐☐ h) Backward roll — straddle
- ☐☐ i) Backward roll to knee scale
- ☐☐ j) Teddy bear stand (see page 25)
- ☐☐ k) Headstand (through tuck position)
- ☐☐ l) Headstand to forward roll out

Dance:
- ☐☐ a) Basic ballet positions
- ☐☐ b) Correct posture and body alignment, arms
- ☐☐ c) Basic locomotor movements: (walking, running, hopping, skipping, jumping, leaping, sliding)

C. NOTES
_____
_____
_____

Uneven Parallel Bars — Level I

A. BASIC REQUIREMENTS
- ☐☐ 1. Long hang
- ☐☐ 2. Front support mount
- ☐☐ 3. Rear dismount
- ☐☐ 4. Straddle over low bar, to stand

B. ADDITIONAL SKILLS
- ☐☐ a) Grips — over, under, mixed, eagle
- ☐☐ b) Beat swing from long hang
- ☐☐ c) Inverted hang low bar (pike position)
- ☐☐ d) Skin the cat
- ☐☐ e) Single knee hock swing (inverted position)

C. NOTES
_____
_____
_____

Balance Beam — Level I

A. BASIC REQUIREMENTS
- ☐☐ 1. Forward walking
- ☐☐ 2. Front support mount to stand
- ☐☐ 3. Knee scale
- ☐☐ 4. Two-foot jumps
- ☐☐ 5. One-half turn on toes of two feet
- ☐☐ 6. Forward roll with spotting
- ☐☐ 7. Straight jump dismount

B. ADDITIONAL SKILLS
- ☐☐ a) Backward walking
- ☐☐ b) V-sit with hands
- ☐☐ c) Tuck jump dismount

C. NOTES
_____
_____
_____

BOOKLET I

Vault — Level I

A. BASIC REQUIREMENTS

☐☐   1.   Squat Vault

B. ADDITIONAL SKILLS

☐☐   a)   Rebound off board onto mats
☐☐   b)   Rebound — tuck
☐☐   c)   Rebound — straddle
☐☐   d)   Rebound — star (arms and legs spread)
☐☐   e)   Rebound — half turn
☐☐   f)   Rebound - full turn
☐☐   g)   In front support position on floor quickly squat between arms on floor — repeat
☐☐   h)   Controlled landing
☐☐   i)   Run squat on-high jump off
☐☐   j)   Squat through
☐☐   k)   Run straddle on

C. NOTES

_____
_____
_____

Floor Exercise — Level II

A. BASIC REQUIREMENTS
- ☐☐ 1. Forward roll — straddle
- ☐☐ 2. Handstand
- ☐☐ 3. Cartwheel
- ☐☐ 4. Chassé (step-together-step)
- ☐☐ 5. Arabesque hop
- ☐☐ 6. Turns on one foot

B. ADDITIONAL SKILLS
- ☐☐ a) Forward roll — full turn
- ☐☐ b) Forward roll walkout
- ☐☐ c) Forward roll one knee tucked under
- ☐☐ d) Straddle arm forward roll forward
- ☐☐ e) Roll no arms
- ☐☐ f) Forward roll to lie on back
- ☐☐ g) Dive forward roll
- ☐☐ h) Dive roll to full twisting jump to dive roll
- ☐☐ i) Backward roll straight legs
- ☐☐ j) Forward roll to half turn to backward roll
- ☐☐ k) Backward roll to knee scale to half turn to splits
- ☐☐ l) Legs together to back straddle
- ☐☐ m) Roll to back straddle to land legs together
- ☐☐ n) Headstand (through pike position)
- ☐☐ o) Headstand (through layout position)
- ☐☐ p) Handstand snap down
- ☐☐ q) Beat cartwheel
- ☐☐ r) Hurdle
- ☐☐ s) Front limber
- ☐☐ t) Back limber

Dance:
- ☐☐ a) Basic locomotor activities with music
- ☐☐ b) Combinations of locomotor activities
- ☐☐ c) Chassé (step-together-step)
- ☐☐ d) Waltz step
- ☐☐ e) Polka step
- ☐☐ f) Arabesque hop
- ☐☐ g) Squat leap

BOOKLET II

- ☐☐ h) Stag leap
- ☐☐ i) Cat leap
- ☐☐ j) Scissors leap
- ☐☐ k) Sissone
- ☐☐ l) Cabriole
- ☐☐ m) Body wave
- ☐☐ n) Turns on two feet
- ☐☐ o) Turns on one foot
- ☐☐ p) Two slide steps to full turn
- ☐☐ q) Pas chassé to kick lunge to full turn
- ☐☐ r) Two slide steps to tour jêté
- ☐☐ s) Pas chassé to kick lunge to full turn

C. NOTES

_____
_____
_____

Uneven Parallel Bars — Level II

A. BASIC REQUIREMENTS
- ☐☐ 1. Pullover mount to front support
- ☐☐ 2. Front support swing to stride support
- ☐☐ 3. Straddle underswing dismount
- ☐☐ 4. Front support swing (cast) on low bar

B. ADDITIONAL SKILLS
- ☐☐ a) Single knee circles — back
- ☐☐ b) Back hip circle low bar
- ☐☐ c) Pike drop from low bar to mat
- ☐☐ d) From sit position on low bar hands on high bar half turn and roll

C. NOTES

_____
_____
_____

Balance Beam — Level II

A. BASIC REQUIREMENTS
- ☐☐ 1. Running forward
- ☐☐ 2. Straddle mount
- ☐☐ 3. Lunge front and side
- ☐☐ 4. Changement
- ☐☐ 5. Tuck jump
- ☐☐ 6. One-half turn on toes of one foot
- ☐☐ 7. Straddle jump dismount

B. ADDITIONAL SKILLS
- ☐☐ a) Forward walking with high kick
- ☐☐ b) Forward walking on toes
- ☐☐ c) Backward walking on toes
- ☐☐ d) Plié walking forward and backward
- ☐☐ e) Step hops
- ☐☐ f) Chassé (step-together-step)
- ☐☐ g) Balances: V-sit without hands
- ☐☐ h) Front scale
- ☐☐ i) Turns: squat turn
- ☐☐ j) Tumbling: back shoulder roll with spotter

C. NOTES

_____

_____

_____

Vault — Level II

A. BASIC REQUIREMENTS
- ☐☐ 1. Straddle Vault

B. ADDITIONAL SKILLS
- ☐☐ a) Side vault

C. NOTES

_____

_____

_____

BOOKLET III

Floor Exercise — Level III

A. BASIC REQUIREMENTS

☐☐ 1. Beginning Floor Exercise Routine
- Sissone (right foot leading)
- Sissone (left foot leading)
- Run
- Cartwheel quarter-turn
- Three back steps to corner
- Stretch on toes
- Bent knee pose
- Quarter-turn to right
- Step kick (on right foot)
- Step kick (on left foot)
- Scissors jump
- Quarter-turn right (same direction)
- Two sliding steps to the right
- Tour jêté to lunge position
- Step forward, full turn on one foot
- Front scale
- Forward roll to stand
- Run
- Round-off
- Backward roll to knee scale
- Pose (optional)

Floor pattern:

B. ADDITIONAL SKILLS

Tumbling:
☐☐ a) Back extension (walkout or snapdown)
☐☐ b) Handstand forward roll
☐☐ c) Handstand to front roll to cartwheel quarter turn
☐☐ d) Headspring on a rolled mat
☐☐ e) Cartwheel quarter-turn to splits
☐☐ f) Cartwheel series
☐☐ g) Round-off
☐☐ h) Running cartwheel
☐☐ i) Round-off half turn round-off
☐☐ j) Round-off to backroll to knee scale
☐☐ k) Combination of any three skills

Dance:
☐☐ a) Chassé split leap
☐☐ b) Tour jêté
☐☐ c) Chassé split leap, split leap
☐☐ d) Waltz step to pique turn
☐☐ e) Combination of three dance movements

C. NOTES

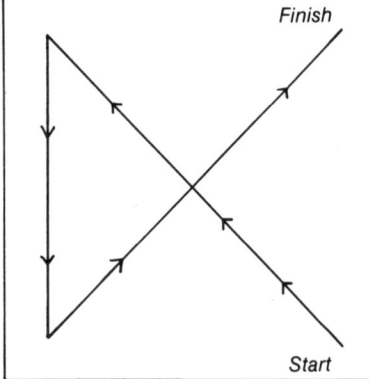

Uneven Parallel Bars — Level III

A. BASIC REQUIREMENTS

☐☐ 1. Beginning Bar Routine:
- Front support mount (facing high bar)
- Stride support
- Single knee drop
- Thigh pivot turn
- Pullover from low bar to high bar
- Pike drop from high bar to low bar
- Straddle underswing dismount

B. ADDITIONAL SKILLS

☐☐ a) Stride circle forward
☐☐ b) Back hip circle high bar
☐☐ c) Stride circle re-grasp

- ☐☐ d) Double leg stem rise to high bar
- ☐☐ e) Hang from high bar, swing into low bar and practice wrap around low bar without releasing hand from high bar (feint wrap)
- ☐☐ f) Shoot to half turn to feint wrap
- ☐☐ g) Pullover to high bar, pike drop to low bar half turn and roll to front support
- ☐☐ h) Cast from low bar into spotter's arms
- ☐☐ i) Cast from high bar into spotter's arms
- ☐☐ j) Cast from high bar to feint wrap

C. NOTES

_____
_____
_____

Balance Beam — Level III

A. BASIC REQUIREMENTS

☐☐ Beginning Balance Beam Routine:
- Squat mount
- Stand bent knee pose
- Quarter-turn to left
- Three back steps to end of beam
- Stretch on toes
- Arabesque (attitude)
- Front scale
- Step-together-step
- High kick to lunge position
- Jump to squat position (back leg in lunge position leads)
- Squat turn
- Tuck jump with height
- Forward roll (support)
- V-sit
- Swing to knee scale
- Stand
- Quarter-turn
- Tuck jump dismount

B. ADDITIONAL SKILLS

- ☐☐ a) Running variations using a variety of speeds and heights
- ☐☐ b) *Mounts:* Single leg mount to squat position
- ☐☐ c) *Balances:* Body wave
- ☐☐ d) *Jumps and leaps:* Changement
- ☐☐ e) Sissone
- ☐☐ f) Scissors leap
- ☐☐ g) Cat leap
- ☐☐ h) *Turns:* Pique turn
- ☐☐ i) Cross over turn
- ☐☐ j) Kick turns
- ☐☐ k) *Tumbling:* Forward roll (support)
- ☐☐ l) Back roll
- ☐☐ m) *Dismounts:* Round-off dismount

C. NOTES

_____
_____
_____

Vault — Level III

A. BASIC REQUIREMENTS

☐☐ 1. Layout squat

B. ADDITIONAL SKILLS

C. NOTES

_____
_____
_____

BOOKLET IV

Floor Exercise — Level IV

A. BASIC REQUIREMENTS

☐☐ 1. Choreograph own routine appropriate for Level IV and minimum of 30 seconds in length, music optional. May use the Level III routine as a start.

B. ADDITIONAL SKILLS

☐☐ a) Headspring
☐☐ b) One armed cartwheel
☐☐ c) Front and back walkovers
☐☐ d) Running walkover
☐☐ e) Back and front walkovers in series
☐☐ f) Tinsica
☐☐ g) Handspring
☐☐ h) Handspring walkout
☐☐ i) Valdez
☐☐ j) Back handspring
☐☐ k) Round-off back handspring
☐☐ l) Round-off back handspring series

C. NOTES

_____

_____

_____

Uneven Parallel Bars — Level IV

A. BASIC REQUIREMENTS

☐☐ 1. Create own uneven bar routine (appropriate for Level IV)

B. ADDITIONAL SKILLS

☐☐ a) Front hip circle low bar
☐☐ b) Front hip circle high bar
☐☐ c) Single leg stem rise
☐☐ d) Front seat circle
☐☐ e) Back seat circle
☐☐ f) Front seat circle re-grasp
☐☐ g) Cast from low bar into spotter's arms
☐☐ h) Cast from high bar into spotter's arms
☐☐ i) Cast from high bar to feint wrap
☐☐ j) Cast from high bar to wrap around low bar

C. ROUTINE AND NOTES

_____

_____

_____

Balance Beam — Level IV

A. BASIC REQUIREMENTS

☐☐ 1. Choreograph own routine minimum two lengths appropriate for Level IV

B. ADDITIONAL SKILLS

Mounts:
☐☐ a) Step on end mount
☐☐ b) Forward roll mount

Balances:
☐☐ c) Splits

Jumps and leaps:
☐☐ d) Split leap

Turns:
☐☐ e) Full turn
☐☐ f) Turns in series

Tumbling:
☐☐ g) Handstand
☐☐ h) Continuous forward roll
☐☐ i) Cartwheel
☐☐ j) Splits
☐☐ k) Walkovers
☐☐ l) Body wave

Dismounts:
☐☐ m) Side handstand dismount quarter turn

C. ROUTINE AND NOTES

_____

_____

_____

Vault — Level IV

A. BASIC REQUIREMENTS

☐☐ 1. Layout straddle vault

B. ADDITIONAL SKILLS

☐☐ a) Headspring
☐☐ b) Stoop vault
☐☐ c) Handspring

C. NOTES

_____
_____
_____

Appendix III
Sample Warm-Up

Sample warm-up for classroom purposes

a) Running
  i) Run on toes, in semi-crouch position.
  ii) Slide, slide, ½ turn.
  iii) Skip — two forward, two backward.
  iv) Gallop.
  v) Jump on two feet.
  vi) Run, run, leap; run, run, leap.

a

b) Dance movements
    Perform a sequence using a waltz step, chassé, full turn, body wave, and polka.

Move to mat or floor
c) Arm flings
    Standing, lock elbows, raise both arms above head and stretch back as far as possible. Then alternate by raising one overhead and then the other.

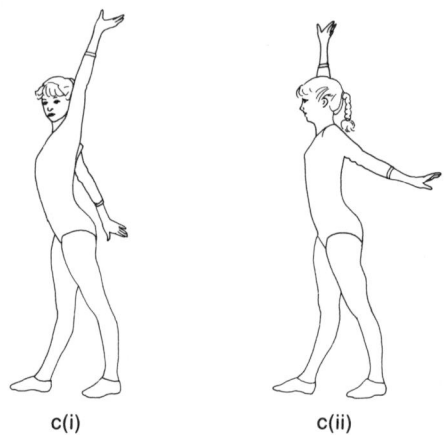

c(i)   c(ii)

d) Rocking chairs
  i) Begin standing, stretch both arms above head.
  ii) Reach for toes with legs straight.
  iii) Squat and reach forward with arms.
  iv) Reach for toes with legs straight.
  v) Return to original position.

d(i)   d(ii)   d(iii)

e) Side lunges
   Point toes directly ahead. Step to side to deep lunge position. Extended leg should be straight. Repeat it five times on each side.

f) Front lunges
   From the side lunge position, turn the body to face bent knee. Extended leg should be straight. Repeat five times on each side.

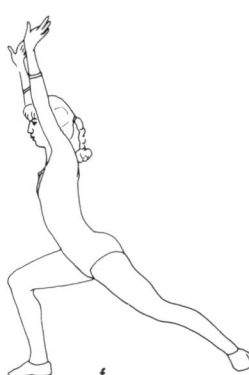

g) Splits Stretch
   From the front lunge position, gradually extend the front leg, lowering the body to a full split position on the floor. The hips and shoulders should be square at all times. Extend feet fully. Practice the splits with the right leg forward and then change position so that the left leg is forward.

Encourage all girls to try splits, even those who are a long way from correctly performing them. Explain that it is better to hold your closest position to splits for a count of five, than not to even attempt it. Arm support is necessary if full splits cannot be done.

Side splits are performed with both legs lateral and should be attempted with care.

h) Straddle stretch
   Begin in a straddle sit position. Place arms to the side and lower *chest* as close to right leg as possible. Repeat to the center and to the opposite leg. Repeat five times for each position.

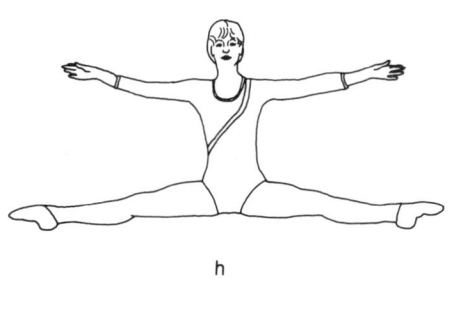

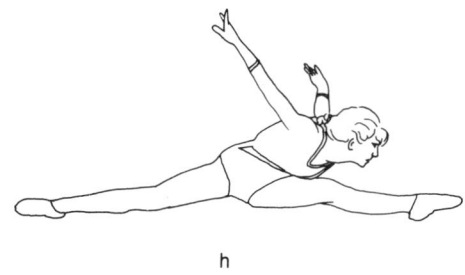

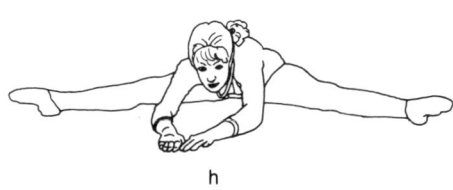

i) Straddle swing to arch
  i) Begin in a straddle sit position, arms extended over left leg.
  ii) Reaching forward as far as possible, move arms over to the right and place right palm on floor beside right hip.
  iii) Lift hip off floor, arching back upwards, head back.
  iv) Simultaneously continue swinging left arm overhead.
  v) Repeat five times on each side, beginning on the right side.
     Encourage an easy relaxed swing and gracefulness. This is a good beginning to warming up the back.

k) Ankle and wrist stretch
  i) From a kneeling position, lower seat to sit on haunches.
  ii) With palms on the floor beside knees and fingers pointing forward, raise the hips upward to a piked position, weight forward on hands.
  iii) Lower to original position. Repeat five times.
     Variation: While in piked position raise one leg and then the other.

k(i)　　　　k(ii)　　　　k(iii)

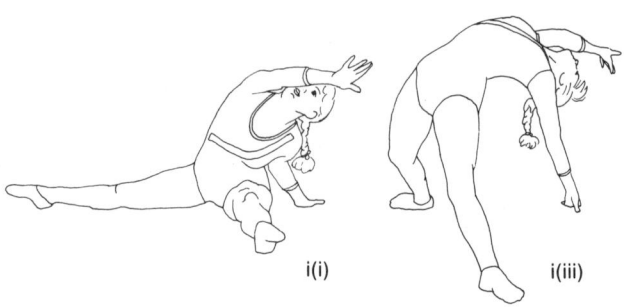

i(i)　　　　　　　i(iii)

l) Neck rotations
   Sit on haunches or cross-legged. Drop the head forward, pause, move to the right, then to the left, and then to the back. Repeat this four times.
   Variation: Rotate the head three times in one continuous motion.

j) Shoulder stretch
  i) Sitting on floor, bring legs together extended forward.
  ii) Place palms on floor behind hips, fingers pointed backward.
  iii) Slide hips forward slowly, stretching arms and shoulders.
  iv) Slide hips back to original position to relax.
     Variation: While in the stretch position, raise legs to V-sit, straddle, and lower to original position.

l

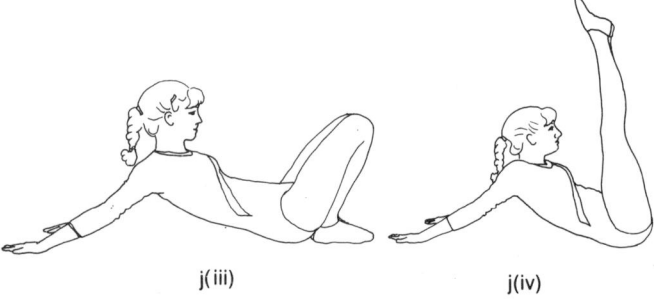

j(iii)　　　　　　j(iv)

m) Wrist rotations
  i) Rotate the hands, going through as wide a range of movement as possible.
  ii) Use the opposite hand to help achieve full extension.

n) Ankle rotations
   i) Rotate the ankles, going through as wide a range of movement as possible.
   ii) Manually rotate one ankle and then the other to help achieve maximum extension.

o) Backbend (Bridge)
   This exercise should be progressive and done slowly.
   i) Begin by lying on the back, knees bent, feet flat on the floor..
   ii) Bend the elbows to place palms on the floor under shoulders, fingers pointing toward toes.
   iii) Raise the body until the top of the head is on the floor, then lower body.
   iv) Raise up a little higher so head is 10 cm. (4") off the floor, and relax.
   v) Repeat until elbows are extended.

Note: For many participants this exercise is very difficult. It should be attempted with care.

Encourage the students to keep both feet flat on the floor (be sure they are not wearing slippery footwear) and to straighten their arms. They should also attempt to straighten their legs and shift their weight over their hands in order to achieve maximum shoulder and upper back extension. Initially the students will have difficulty knowing in which direction to shift the weight while in the inverted position. The instructor or a partner may assist by gently pulling the performer toward her.

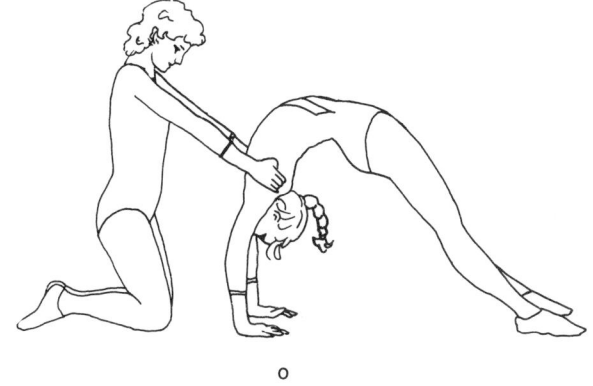

o

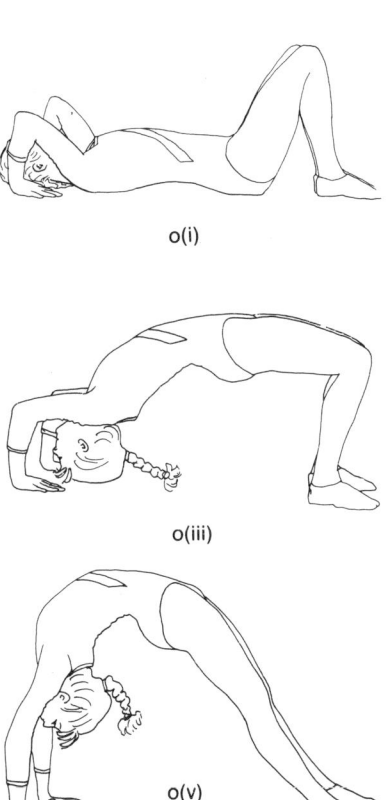

o(i)

o(iii)

o(v)

Appendix IV
Glossary

Aerial: Skill performed without hands — body suspended in the air.

Amplitude: Degree or amount of movement away from the stationary position. Swings with low amplitude move only a few degrees away from the stationary position. Judges look for amplitude in leg lifts and jumps. The higher the leg lift or the jump, the greater the amplitude is said to be.

Arched: The back is hyperextended, head is back, abdomen forward.

Back bend: Also called bridge. Back is facing floor, hands and feet supporting body in an arched position.

Back flip: Also called back salto or back somersault. Backward aerial movement performed in a tuck position. Same skill can be performed forward — front flip.

Beat board: Also called Reuther Board. Device used for vaulting or for mounting the balance beam or the uneven bars.

B.C.G.A.: British Columbia Gymnastics Association, the governing body for all clubs in the province of B.C.

C.G.F.: Canadian Gymnastics Federation, the governing body for all provinces.

Code of Points: Judging booklets written by F.I.G. There are separate men's and women's Codes of Points. Available through C.G.F.

Correct Form: Performing the skill correctly.

Crash pad: Large foam rubber mat used for cushioning dismounts or for added protection when performing new skills.

Demi-plié: Slight knee bend.

Dismount: The last skill in a routine or series of skills.

Element: Skill, trick.

Etendre: To stretch

Extended: Stretched to maximum position, straight.

Execution: How the skill is performed.

F.I.G. Federation of International Gymnastics, the international governing body.

Flexed: Bent.

Glissé: To glide.

Inverted: Upside down.

Jêté: Small hop or jump.

Layout: Straight body position. May have a slight arch in aerial movements.

Lead-up: One or more skills progressing to a more difficult skill. Used in a teaching progression.

Medium Difficulty: Classification of skills, according to difficulty. Established by F.I.G.

Mount: The first skill of a routine or series of skills.

Orientation: Getting the "feel" of a particular skill or position.

Pike: Hips flexed, upper body bent forward, legs together and straight.

Pirouette: Rotating around the long axis of the body. A full turn in the air while the feet are off the floor. Also known as a twist.
May also be a full turn in the air without support of the hands as on the uneven bars.

Plié: Fully bending the knees. To bend.

Pivot: Turn on the ball of the foot.

"Pop":	Refers to a very explosive movement on the uneven bars. A sudden lifting motion.
Prone:	Lying face down.
Releve:	To raise.
Saute:	To jump.
Scale:	A balance, arabesque.
Side Box:	Also called cross box: vaulting crosswise instead of lengthwise.
Squat:	Knees to the chest, feet flat on the floor.
Straddle:	Legs separated sideways.
Stride:	Legs separated, one forward, one backward.
Superior Movement:	Classification by difficulty established by F.I.G.
Supine:	Lying on back, face up.
Support Roll:	On the balance beam a support roll is a roll where the gymnast supports herself by grasping the beam in the inverted position to maintain her balance. The word "support" in this case does not refer to spotting.
Swedish Box:	This is a four-sectional wooden box with a padded leather top. The sections can be removed to lower the height.
Tourner:	To turn.
Tuck:	Knees bent, close to the chest.

Notes

Notes

Sports Handbook Series

Tennis Handbook
Graphics illustrate grips and strokes in this compact guide to a popular sport. Everything necessary to teach - and play - is tucked between the covers.
ISBN 0-88839-049-1

Folk Dance Handbook
The fascinating complexities of this activity are set out in a clear, easy-to-follow format that should bring the delights of folk dance within the reach of everyone.
ISBN 0-88839-044-0

Soccer Handbook
Skills and how to teach them; drills and when to use them; plus detailed plans for sequential teaching of the game. Compact yet comprehensive.
ISBN 0-88839-048-3

Field Hockey Handbook
Concise, clearly illustrated, a useful guide to learning and teaching a fast-growing sport.
ISBN 0-88839-043-2

Basketball Handbook
Rules and activities are clearly illustrated to make this guide indispensable to anyone coaching or teaching the game.
ISBN 0-88839-042-4

Badminton Handbook
A well-illustrated guide to all the basics of the game, this also includes a discussion of teaching strategies when player skills vary widely.
ISBN 0-88839-041-6

Men's Gymnastics Handbook
Teaching sequences for the six Olympic events of men's artistic gymnastics are explained in detail, with precise information on spotting and safety techniques providing valuable guidance for the instructor.
ISBN 0-88839-046-7

Women's Gymnastics Handbook
A detailed guide to the teaching of gymnastic skills for women, including lesson plans and methods for evaluating performers.
ISBN 0-88839-045-9

Orienteering Handbook
The rapidly-growing interest in this activity makes the publication of this book particularly timely. It includes detailed information on basic concepts, setting a course and organizing a meet, as well as addresses for obtaining equipment and other resources.
ISBN 0-88839-047-5